"I consider Ruth Haley Barton a treasured gift to the church! Ruth knows what she is talking about. Her mind, heart, and soul shine on the pages of *Embracing Rhythms of Work and Rest*. Ruth is a rare, trustworthy guide for the person in need of deep rest."

Todd Hunter, bishop, Churches for the Sake of Others, and author of *Deep Peace: Finding Calm in a World of Conflict and Anxiety*

"In the face of the demographic shifts and national divisions happening in our world today, many leaders are often frustrated, fatigued, and despondent, desperately searching for a different way forward. That is exactly what Ruth Haley Barton offers us in this groundbreaking, new book *Embracing Rhythms of Work and Rest*. This is an invitation for leaders to take the next step into sabbath living that gives them life and longevity in ministry. It is also a prophetic wake-up call, leading us away from individualism into the communal practice of sabbath keeping as it was always meant to be. I highly recommend this book for all those who deeply desire to find a new way of life together in community that brings true healing and wholeness. I could not be more excited for this much-needed and timely book!"

Brenda Salter McNeil, author of *Becoming Brave* and *Roadmap to Reconciliation 2.0: Moving Communities into Unity, Wholeness and Justice*

"In her new book *Embracing Rhythms of Work and Rest*, Ruth Haley Barton masterfully explores the sabbath tradition within our modern context and re-centers this practice on God. Sharing anecdotes from her own personal journey, Barton beautifully captures the joy of the sabbath we see in Scripture and provides a practical approach to reclaiming the gift of rest, not only in our own lives but in our communities as well."

D. Michael Lindsay, president of Taylor University and author of *Hinge Moments: Making the Most of Life's Transitions*

"Ruth Barton is that rare Christian leader who not only preaches about the sabbath, she practices it weekly. Her delight in the sabbath and her love for it are contagious. I dare you to read about Ruth's journey with the sabbath and not fall in love with it yourself. I guarantee this book will awaken a desire in you to set aside work and to rest in God for one day each week, not as an obligation but out of sheer delight. May you discover the joy of sabbath-keeping as a way of life."

Rory Noland, director of Heart of the Artist Ministries and author of *Transforming Worship: Planning and Leading Sunday Services as If Spiritual Formation Mattered*

"This book will stir up a longing to receive one of God's greatest gifts to his children—the gift of sabbath rest. Ruth Haley Barton has been a guide to so many leaders, including me, to make intentional and radical choices in order to live a sustainable life. A picture of such a life is painted here with the wisdom of Scripture and practical examples, in the stories of real people who deal with children, jobs, bills to pay, and the pervasive intrusion of technology. I came away believing a healthy rhythm is both possible and deeply desirable."

Nancy Beach, leadership coach and coauthor with Samantha Beach Kiley of *Next Sunday: An Honest Dialogue About the Future of the Church*

"In *Embracing Rhythms of Work and Rest*, Ruth Haley Barton invites us into a holy place—what Rabbi Abraham Joshua Heschel called 'a sanctuary in time.' Barton profoundly weaves together disparate strands of the practice of sabbath-keeping into a beautiful quilt that tells us a story about ourselves—we were meant for wholeness, not just individually, but communally. *Embracing Rhythms of Work and Rest* shows us that this gift from God is not just indispensable for the life of faith but also in our discovery of what it means to be human. Barton has given us a treasure—a must-read for anyone longing for freedom from the tyranny of endless work and overproduction."

Drew Jackson, poet and author of *God Speaks Through Wombs*

"Do you know it takes courage to rest? Ruth Haley Barton has written a gentle, compassionate, and life-giving book on the beauty and healing that can be found in sabbath rest. Learning from her wisdom and practical guidance, we can stop striving and start resting in our God's good presence and grace. Read this and receive not just the permission to rest from work but to learn the joy of resting *in* God."

Kelly M. Kapic, author of *You're Only Human* and *Embodied Hope*

"For leaders who care as much about the state of their souls as the fruitfulness of their service, Ruth Haley Barton could be the most trusted advisor. Her wisdom, experience, and honesty shines through and offers an example of the challenge of developing a deeply rooted, healthy way of living and leading. *Embracing Rhythms of Work and Rest* offers spiritual guidance for leaders who know deep in their bones that they need a way of being that is more intentional, reflective, practical, and restorative. Take a deep breath, be prepared for all that will be stirred up, and then bask in the teaching of this profoundly beautiful book."

Tod Bolsinger, author of *Tempered Resilience: How Leaders Are Formed in the Crucible of Change*

"She's done it again. For many years now, Ruth Haley Barton has been a trustworthy guide—for the church at large and for leaders in particular—on deep formation and flourishing from the inside out. In this magnificent work, she turns her focus to sabbaths and sabbaticals. Shaped by Scripture, theology, and the wisdom borne from a life of practice, Barton knows when to challenge us, confronting our idols and addictions, and when to encourage us, giving us hope to believe that change and healing are possible. This is a foundational book fit for the challenges of today's world."

Glenn Packiam, pastor and author of *The Resilient Pastor* and *Blessed Broken Given*

EMBRACING

RHYTHMS

of

WORK

and

REST

From Sabbath to
Sabbatical and
Back Again

Foreword by Ronald Rolheiser

RUTH HALEY BARTON

An imprint of InterVarsity Press
Downers Grove, Illinois

InterVarsity Press
P.O. Box 1400 | Downers Grove, IL 60515-1426
ivpress.com | email@ivpress.com

InterVarsity Press® is the publishing division of InterVarsity Christian Fellowship/USA®.
For more information, visit intervarsity.org.

Scripture quotations, unless otherwise noted, are from the New Revised Standard Version Bible, copyright © 1989 National Council of the Churches of Christ in the United States of America. Used by permission. All rights reserved worldwide.

While any stories in this book are true, some names and identifying information may have been changed to protect the privacy of individuals.

The publisher cannot verify the accuracy or functionality of website URLs used in this book beyond the date of publication.

Cover design and image composite: David Fassett
Interior design: Jeanna Wiggins

ISBN 978-1-5140-0263-6 (print) | ISBN 978-1-5140-0264-3 (digital)

Library of Congress Cataloging-in-Publication Data
A catalog record for this book is available from the Library of Congress.

29 28 27 26 25 24 23 22 | 8 7 6 5 4 3 2 1

FOR MY FAMILY—

the best part of any sabbath

AND FOR THE TRANSFORMING CENTER,

who has given me the gift of sabbatical—more than once—

with such love and generosity.

It is one of the main reasons I am still here!

● ● ●

Because we do not rest, we lose our way.

WAYNE MULLER

CONTENTS

FOREWORD

RONALD ROLHEISER

THERE IS A KIND OF HURRY that is a form of violence exercised upon time that is detrimental to our health, to our families, to our communities, and to our relationship with God. Admittedly, there are times when the demands of relationships, family, work, school, church, childcare, shopping, health, appearance, housework, meals, bill payments, commuting, accidents, interruptions, illnesses, and countless other things eat up more time than is seemingly available. Living under pressure is part of life. Still we have to be careful not to rationalize. God didn't make a mistake in creating time; God made enough of it. When we cannot find enough time and, as the psalmist says, find ourselves getting up earlier and going to bed later because we have too much to do, we can see this as a sign to make some changes in our lives. When we allow ourselves to be driven like this for too long, we end up doing violence to time, to ourselves, and to our blood pressure.

What's the answer? There is no simple answer, but there is a divinely given counsel regarding how we can prevent ourselves from becoming addicted to pressure and rushing headlong through our lives. Indeed, it's more than counsel to lower blood pressure, it's one of the Ten Commandments: *Remember to keep holy the sabbath day.*

When we look at this, the fourth commandment, it is more profitable to ask what is *bidden* by it rather than what is *forbidden* by it. What is the positive challenge of God telling us to rest one day a week?

For most of us, I suspect, the fourth commandment has simply meant that we could not do our normal work on Sundays and that we are encouraged to go to church that day. Until recently, Western culture played along and most non-vital businesses and commerce shut down on Sundays. Moreover, if we transgressed, we quickly confessed: "I missed going to church" or "I worked on Sunday."

Today, there's a lot of confusion about what it means to keep the sabbath day holy. Worse still, for the most part, this commandment is simply ignored. As Wayne Muller points out, we have turned a commandment into a lifestyle suggestion. More and more, it's business as usual on Sundays; many of us are obliged to work on that day, church attendance is declining steadily, and we are living increasingly pressured lives.

In light of all of this, we need to ask again, *What does it mean to keep holy the sabbath day?*

It means more things than we imagine. In this much-needed book, Ruth Haley Barton gives us a theology, spirituality, and anthropology of sabbath, explicating what sabbath means, why it is so important in our lives, and how we might practice it today inside all the pressures of our lives. Furthermore, she calls us to consider the communal nature of sabbath-keeping so that our life together in communities supports and catalyzes this key practice of our Christian faith.

Addressing leaders regarding their role in leading communities that practice together, Barton makes it clear that observing sabbath is critical, religiously and psychologically. Unless we pull back from our normal lives regularly to rest, worship, and forgive, we will lose perspective on what is ultimately important and become compulsive, driven, hurrying persons caught up in pressure—ambitious, greedy, resentful, unable to pray, unable to forgive, and unable to simply enjoy life. It's no accident that as sabbath observance is slipping today, we find ourselves feeling ever more trapped and more pressured, always behind, never really able to rest deeply, and less able to delight in the deep joys of life.

Good leaders seek to receive sabbath as a gift in their own lives and are faithful to share that gift with others. We need to reground ourselves in a spirituality of sabbath.

God gave us the sabbath. Jesus taught us that we weren't made for the sabbath but that sabbath was made for us. Ruth Haley Barton reminds us that sabbath time is our time, our chance to rest, to worship God, to forgive each other, to taste a wee bit of heaven, and to be more in sympathy with all that is, not least our own lives.

Part One

SABBATH

1

A WAKE-UP CALL

* * *

Sabbath is the most precious present humankind
has received from the treasure house of God.

ABRAHAM JOSHUA HESCHEL

I AM QUITE CERTAIN I would not be alive today if it were not for God's gift of sabbath. And not just a weekly sabbath day, but also daily sabbath moments cultivated in solitude and silence, and sabbatical seasons for letting the soil of my soul lie fallow. These rhythms have given shape and form to a life—my life—lived as a creature in the presence of my loving Creator; these sabbath rhythms have, quite literally, kept me in the game.

But I have not always lived this way.

My wake-up call regarding God's gift of sabbath came when I was in my early forties, serving on staff in a high-performance church culture, married with three busy and athletic children, writing, teaching, and guiding others in spiritual practices, and yet . . . I was actively resisting sabbath. I knew sabbath was a thing. But on a level I had not yet been willing to acknowledge, I was too busy, too important, too caught in cultural expectations, to consider ceasing my work one day a week. In addition to my grandiosity, the logistics of family life and work made it all seem just beyond our reach. Sunday was the only day it was even possible for our busy family to attempt a sabbath, yet traveling sports teams competed on Sundays, my husband's place of work was open on Sundays, and my own job on a church staff made Sunday the busiest day of my work week! Sigh.

The deeper truth is that I just wasn't that attracted to sabbath as a concept. I had been raised in a fundamentalist environment where sabbath *was* kept, but in a very legalistic way. For me, sabbath had been a day of contradictions. We went to church in the morning and since my dad was the pastor we kids had to work very hard at behaving. Sitting in the front row knowing people were watching us from behind while our dad watched us eagle-eyed from the pulpit was stressful, to say the least. Even the most minor infraction (like giggling or whispering) was treated with great seriousness when we got home. This was not restful or delightful at all.

Added to this was the fact that as the pastor's family we often had guests for dinner or were guests at someone else's home most Sundays after church. I enjoyed the communal nature of the hospitality that was part of our sabbath routine (in fact, I still miss it!), but I will say that the womenfolk—including myself as "the responsible eldest"—worked very hard at cooking, serving, and cleaning up while the menfolk visited in the living room. In fact, I'm not sure there was any other day of the week in which we women worked harder than we did on that day; it didn't take long for me to grow resentful.

Our guests usually stayed through the afternoon, so we remained in our "Sunday clothes" all day, were limited in what we were allowed to do (no biking or swimming), and then it was back to church in the evening. All in all, sabbath was pretty exhausting and slightly punishing, so when I left for college and eventually established my own family, I was glad to leave that particular brand of sabbath-keeping behind. It was convenient to dismiss it as a practice we didn't need to worry about anymore—not to mention the fact that as a young adult I was really into working and achieving, and Sundays were a day when I could get a lot done. I was so driven by my goals and aspirations that I really did not want to stop—for anything or anybody, including God! That is, until years later I was so tired from my overachieving ways that in unguarded moments I started dreaming of a way of life that was not so exhausting.

I developed a bit of a guilty pleasure—reading beautiful books about the sabbath, allowing the longing to well up within me for a few minutes, living inside the fantasy for just a bit, and then setting the book aside as a private indulgence full of pleasures I could imagine for others but not myself. I kept my explorations to myself because I wanted to dream without interruption—at least for a little while. I did not want the naysayers telling me sabbath-keeping was not possible.

By this time I had been to seminary and understood the basic hermeneutical principle that if you want to know what matters to God, you look for the great themes of Scripture, the arc if you will. The way I saw it, the theme of sabbath and rest was a vibrant thread running throughout Scripture—I had no patience for theologically resistant folks raising questions about whether or not sabbath-keeping is for today and why

Jesus didn't teach about the sabbath. To my knowledge God had never "taken back" the gift of the sabbath—it was one of the Ten Commandments, after all, and the best one if you ask me!

It seemed to me that Jesus never taught about sabbath because it was just assumed: as practicing Jews, he and his disciples kept the sabbath and that was that. Yes, he brought fresh nuance to it by making it clear that the sabbath was made for humankind and not humankind for the sabbath, *and* that he is Lord even of the sabbath (Mark 2:27). So rather than doing away with it, he actually rescued it from legalism, reframing it in such a way that it is even more life-giving for us as his followers. And then, to put an even finer point on it, the writer of Hebrews stated in no uncertain terms that the promise of sabbath rest is still available to the people of God and that to refuse such rest is to harden one's heart in disobedience (Hebrews 4:9).

So, while I longed for this kind of rest and was completely convinced of its importance, biblically speaking, I did not want to wrestle with all the complications and practical challenges just yet. Somehow, just knowing the possibility of sabbath existed and that somebody somewhere was able to figure out how to have it, lit up my soul from the inside. Yet it still felt impossible for me.

STOPPED IN MY TRACKS

Then I had this biking accident—one I now see as something similar to God knocking Paul off his horse and leaving him alone and sightless for three days so he could ponder his life. I will refrain from retelling that whole story here, except to say that after the initial euphoria of having survived such a thing wore off, I went right back to work. But as relief gave way to other levels of awareness, God used a couple comments to help me ponder the meaning of things. One friend, after expressing his initial concern, laughingly commented, "Ruth, when are you going to learn that when you're on a bike, you can't take on a van?" Another friend, curious about the fact that I wasn't taking any time to recover, commented, "You know, you did just get run over by a car. You could take a day off!"

And then there was this sentence from Wayne Muller's book *Sabbath* that kept buzzing around in my head like a pesky fly buzzing against a windowpane: "If we do not allow for a rhythm of rest in our overly busy lives, illness becomes our Sabbath— our pneumonia, our cancer, our heart attack, our accidents create Sabbath for us."

Boom.

I did not want to hear this. I did not want to consider the fact that perhaps this accident, while not God's fault, was a way in which God was trying to tell me something. I did not want to acknowledge the possibility that it might be that hard for God to get my attention; nor did I want to face the fact that for years I had been thumbing my nose at human limitations, behaving as though I was beyond needing a sabbath. It was a nice idea for retired people or people who weren't in demand, but surely *I* wasn't one who *needed* a sabbath.

Except now I did.

And that is how God began nudging me to take next steps on my sabbath journey. Unbeknownst to me, my sabbath journey had already begun because I had been practicing solitude in a profoundly different way than the busy "quiet times" I had been schooled in during my youth. Through the witness of the desert Abbas and Ammas (particularly Henri Nouwen's seminal reflections in *The Way of the Heart*), I had been learning how to cultivate solitude as a place of rest in God—body, mind, and soul. It was wonderful. It was restful. It was bringing me back to life. Little did I know that in my practice of solitude and silence, I was already experiencing what Tilden Edwards calls "a special *quality of time* available daily"—a way of being in time that is open and receptive, restful and replenishing.

God used my accident to stop me in my tracks—to provide the right kind of space to really consider my human limitations and the layers of exhaustion that existed within me. In this space I was able to stay with my desire for a more sustainable existence long enough for it to take me somewhere. Even though I do not believe God caused the accident, I *do* believe the Holy One used it to get my attention and draw me into his invitation to take a next step in sabbath living—from a few delicious sabbath moments daily to a full day once a week, and then eventually longer sabbatical seasons—until here I am today, able to testify that God's gift of sabbath is far more than just one day a week; it is actually a *way of life*.

A SANCTUARY IN TIME

Sabbath-keeping is a way of ordering all of life around a pattern of working six days and then ceasing and resting on the seventh. It helps us arrange our lives to honor the rhythm of things—work and rest, fruitfulness and dormancy, giving and receiving, being and doing, activism and surrender. The day itself is set apart, devoted completely to rest, worship, and delighting in God's good gifts, but the other six days of the week must be lived in such a way as to make sabbath possible. Paid work needs to be contained within five days a week. Household chores, shopping, and errand running need to be completed before the sabbath comes or they need to wait. Courageous decisions must be made about work and athletics, church and community involvement.

This pattern of tithing one-seventh of our time back to God is woven deep into the fabric of Christian tradition. It is a pattern God himself established as he was doing the work of creation, and it was incorporated into Jewish tradition in such a way that it ordered their whole existence as a nation. For Jewish folks, the sabbath observance began on Friday evening and ended on Saturday evening, providing a sanctuary in time even during seasons in their history when they had no physical sanctuary. The practice of keeping the sabbath holy and completely set apart was and still is at the heart of their national identity. "It was as if a whole people were in love with the seventh day."

I have experienced this love myself in the joy and relief that washes over me when sabbath comes . . . when the house has been prepared, special food has been bought, computers have been turned off and cellphones powered down . . . when final emails have been sent and the laptop has been closed, when work obligations have been completed or set aside . . . when the candles or the fireplace have been lit . . . and it is time to stop, whether everything has been finished or not. I know what it is like to rest for hours until I have energy to delight in something—savory food, a good book, a leisurely walk, a long-awaited conversation with someone I love. I know what it's like to feel joy, hope, and peace flow back into my body and soul when I thought it might never come back again. I know what it's like to see home and family, friends and community, differently through sabbath eyes of delight in God's good gifts. I have experienced rest that turns into delight, delight that turns into gratitude, and gratitude that turns into worship. I know what it is like to recover myself so completely that I am able, by God's grace, to enter back into my work with a renewed sense of God's calling and God's presence.

How could you not love a day that does all that? How could you not sell everything you have for this pearl of great price?

A SABBATH PROGRESSION

If you ask me, sabbath is one of God's greatest gifts to us in our humanity—right up there with salvation through Christ. It is a gift that is both beautiful *and* functional, luxurious *and* essential all at the same time. And every time you open it, it feels brand new.

For me, sabbath-keeping has been a progression that started with cultivating a daily practice of solitude and silence as a place of rest in God, where I began to experience *for the first time* what it felt like to cease striving, to give in to the limits of being human, and to rest myself upon God's care and mercy. What an amazing experience this was for one who had worked so hard on so many things—including my spirituality—for so long. In the process I became more aware of my drivenness and how deeply entrenched it was. I had to really own the propensities of my personality and say, "Yes, this is what's true about me." Sitting uncomfortably with that admission, I could finally get honest about just how tired I was—deep in my bones—and this awareness prepared me to really hear God's invitation to set aside my work and my ceaseless striving for an entire day once a week. These shorter, daily periods of resting in God in solitude gave me a taste of what could be.

As my capacity to let go and cease striving increased through this daily practice of solitude and silence, God drew me back to the biblical practice of a whole day set apart for rest, worship, and delight—a practice I had rejected but now God was returning to me in the most winsome way. Now I wanted it badly enough that I was willing to do pretty much anything to get it.

There were several fundamental principles that got me started with my sabbath practice—all of which we will explore in different ways throughout this book. The first was really digging in and seeking to understand God's heart and intention in giving us the sabbath—that we as his children would experience this rhythm of ceasing and resting, worshiping and delighting. Eventually it dawned on me that everything we choose to do or not do needs to somehow fit into *God's purposes* for this day. There is so much to this that it will take the first half of this book to plumb the depths!

The second principle is that it is important to establish a regular rhythm if at all possible. The human body and soul is accustomed to living in rhythms—rhythms of night and day, rhythms of the seasons, rhythms of eating three meals a day, and so on. Part of the restfulness of sabbath is knowing that it always comes at the same interval so we're not making decisions about it every week. When sabbath is not observed on the same day every week, there will be weeks when we go longer than seven days without a sabbath, and that is not optimal. After seven days without rest, we risk becoming dangerously tired and unable to bring our best selves to anyone or anything.

Third, I eventually grasped that sabbath-keeping is not primarily a private discipline. It is and always has been a communal discipline or at least a discipline to be entered into with those closest to us. After experiencing church communities that ramp up their activities on Sundays versus guiding their people into sabbath rhythms, I could see that the reason sabbath worked in the Jewish community is that they all did it together. The communal nature of sabbath is such an important topic that we will devote an entire chapter to it later on. But having these foundational principles was enough to get me started.

FALLING IN LOVE GRADUALLY

Jewish folks had it right: the only way to even begin taking steps toward a sabbath practice is to let yourself fall in love with this day so that you long for it as you would long for a loved one. Rabbi Heschel puts it this way: "There is a word that is seldom said, a word for an emotion almost too deep to be expressed: the love of the Sabbath. The word is rarely found in our literature, yet for more than two thousand years the emotion filled our songs and moods. It was as if a whole people were in love with the seventh day." This beautiful perspective has guided me to resist making sabbath-keeping a weighty exercise but to fall in love gradually—to explore it with delight—as though God and I were learning how to spend time together in a new and special way.

Falling in love with the sabbath does not mean it is always easy or that I have never given in to the temptation to pursue my own interests on God's holy day (Isaiah 58:13). But twenty years later, I *can* say that I am a passionate lover of the sabbath who would not be standing in the middle of my life and calling today if it weren't for this essential rhythm. The journey has continued to unfold as God has invited me into longer periods of retreat, and then finally into embracing sabbatical as part and parcel of my sabbath life in leadership.

A particular delight was discovering that I can bring this special quality of time into my everyday life through "sabbath pauses." I could take a moment to rest in God between one activity and the next. I could pause before entering a room or a new situation to orient myself to God and invite God's presence. Before meals I could sometimes create space for a moment of quiet gratitude rather than just offering up a perfunctory prayer. While waiting for an appointment I could choose to cease and just be instead of scrolling through the apps on my phone. I could use time in the car or on a walk to be still and allow God to replenish me rather than turning on music or podcasts or making phone calls. All of these are simple means of introducing a sabbath way of being into other days and moments of the week, affirming that sabbath is a *quality-of-time* way of being that is possible anytime, anywhere.

Taken together, this sabbath progression has kept me navigating within sane rhythms of work, rest, and renewal for long-term sustainability. It all starts with longing and love as we allow ourselves to get in touch with the desire that stirs deep within our soul—desire for a way of life that works. A way of life in which we are not so tired all the time. A way of life that recognizes, accepts, and even honors the limits of our humanity, fostering contentment through delighting in God's truest gifts. When we are brave enough to be in touch with this stirring of the soul, God meets us right there in the middle of our desire with the revelation of this amazing gift that is fitted perfectly for us. Then we simply say yes to a God who knows us so well and loves us so much that he has provided us with such a good gift—if we can just arrange our lives to receive it.

The encouragement to "simply say yes" is not to imply that sabbath-keeping is easy; it is not. In fact, sabbath-keeping has only gotten more complicated as our culture has moved away from distinguishing any one day as different from the rest. And the ubiquitous nature of technology has added layers of challenge and difficulty to the prospect of unplugging and resting from constant connection and stimulation.

To enter sabbath time despite all the challenges, there must be a real yes, deep down inside. Yes to our need, yes to our desperation, yes to God's invitation and the rightness of it—before we even know how we're going to make it real in our own lives. This is the very definition of faith—to say yes when we have no idea how it's all going to work out, but we know it's what we need to do. It is that deep interior yes that will carry us into and through all the knotty issues sabbath raises until we emerge with a sabbath practice that works. There really is no shortcut, no other way, except through the doorway of desire, accompanied by faith that God is calling us and will show us the way. In this process, we learn for ourselves that yes, indeed, the sabbath *is* the most precious present humankind has received from the treasure house of God.

EMBRACING SABBATH TOGETHER

Because it takes whole communities embracing sabbath together to ensure that we can all participate in this God-ordained way of life, in this book I am unabashedly addressing pastors and leaders of churches and ministries who gather in Jesus' name. Sabbath communities do not happen by accident; they must be led by leaders who are practicing sabbath themselves so they have the inner authority to guide others. And then these sabbath principles need to be lived into with others so that our shared life supports and catalyzes this practice rather than working against it.

In part one we explore the personal and communal practice of a weekly sabbath as foundational to a way of life that works and honors the God who made us. We conclude with the story of Pastor Dan and how God stirred in his heart and life to lead his community in embracing sane rhythms of work and rest together. Then in part two we explore the practice of sabbatical as an extension of our sabbath practice. There are many practical tools for sabbath and sabbatical offered throughout the book, including a conversation guide for communities seeking to explore becoming a sabbath community. Knowing about this communal emphasis, you may want to consider reading and engaging this work with a few other leaders in your community who have the desire, will, and capacity to move forward on this with you.

But first, let's take a few moments to pay attention to what is stirring deep within our own souls as we reflect on God's invitation to sabbath. Someone has said, "You'd be surprised what your soul wants to say to God." And, I might add, "You'd be surprised what God wants to say to your soul." At the end of each chapter, there is a section intended to create space for letting yourself be surprised by what your soul wants to say to God *and* to keep the space open long enough to listen for what God wants to say back to your soul.

What Your Soul Wants to Say to God

Desire is the language of the soul and every spiritual practice corresponds to some deep desire of the human heart. The practice of sabbath corresponds to the human desire for rest and replenishment. Freedom. Delight. A way of life that works. The commitment to actually embrace a sabbath life (rather than just reading about it, as I did for a while) emerges from a deep connection with our own souls and the desires that stir there, so we can eventually say something true to God about it. Here you can let your response to what you have read flow freely, and then sit quietly to listen for what God wants to say about how you can live a sabbath life. I pray you will not skip this part, because the best and most consistent practice always emerges from being in touch with our truest desires and then seeking to order our lives from that place. So go ahead and express the desire that stirs in response to this reading. Speak to God directly, in whatever words are coming to you right now.

Also, reflect on your own history with sabbath-keeping. How did you first learn about the sabbath, and who taught you? Are those early voices still with you, and what do they say? If you do not have any history with sabbath-keeping, name that as well.

What insight emerges as you reflect on this history from your current vantage point? And what is God's invitation to you now?

2

BEGINNING *with* GOD

• • •

*There is a realm of time where the goal is not to
have but to be, not to own but to give, not to control
but to share, not to subdue but to be in accord.*

ABRAHAM JOSHUA HESCHEL

ONE OF THE WAYS I got around sabbath-keeping for so long
is that I dismissed it as "a Jewish thing" that had very little to
do with me. It was certainly a nice idea, but I wasn't convinced
it was something important from God *for me.* I am not alone in
this; it seems many have had a tendency to dismiss sabbath as
being part of another culture, a relic of another place and time.
This is why it is so important to begin our exploration of the
sabbath by fully grasping that this whole idea actually begins
with God. God lived it first and later shared it with his chosen
people as the optimal way to live.

When time had no shape at all, God created "a holiness in
time" by working six days and then ceasing on the seventh. Over
time this rhythm became uniquely associated with the Jewish

17

culture because the Israelites were the first group of people to practice sabbath and experience its benefits, but the pattern of working six days and then resting on the seventh is something that flows from God's very nature and being. So we honor those who first incorporated sabbath-keeping into their way of life and learn all we can from them (which certainly puts the Judeo back into our Judeo-Christian tradition!), knowing that the practice of sabbath-keeping really cannot be relegated to one group of people in one time period. Sabbath begins with God.

MORE THAN A LIFESTYLE SUGGESTION

Sabbath is more than a lifestyle suggestion or an expression of one's ethnicity. It is a spiritual precept that emerges from the creation narrative where God expresses God's very nature by finishing the work and then ceasing on the seventh day. In an article about Shabbat, the Jewish Sabbath, George Robinson writes:

> In the Torah it is written, "On the seventh day God finished the work . . . and ceased from all the work . . . and God blessed the seventh day and declared it holy, because on it God ceased from all the work of creation" (Genesis 2:2-3). But what did God create on the seventh day? Didn't God "cease from all the work of Creation" on the seventh day? What God created on the seventh day, the ancient rabbis tell us, was rest.

Rabbi Abraham Heschel in his seminal work, *The Sabbath,* elaborates:

> After the six days of creation—what did the universe still lack? *Menuha*. Came the Sabbath, came *menuha,* and the universe was complete. *Menuha* which we usually render

18

with "rest," means here much more than withdrawal from labor and exertion, more than freedom from toil, strain or activity of any kind. *Menuha* is not a negative concept but something real and intrinsically positive. . . . What was created on the seventh day? *Tranquility, serenity, peace* and *repose*. To the biblical mind *menuha* is the same as happiness and stillness, as peace and harmony.

What a thrilling thought! What if rest has already been created and all I have to do is find ways to participate? What if God has already done the work of creating this sanctuary in time and all I have to do is enter in? What if, on this one day a week, I am freed to cease my own work and productivity and can simply be at one with all that has already been created? And if this pattern of working six days and then entering into tranquility and peace, happiness and harmony on the seventh has always been there for us—established by God at the very beginning of the created order—how might this change our lives if we fully grasped its significance?

George Robinson continues:

Shabbat offers us a chance for peace with nature, with society, and with ourselves. The prohibitions on work are designed to make us stop—if only for one day a week—our relentless efforts to tame, to conquer, to subdue the earth and everything on it. The prohibition against making fire is also said by the rabbis to mean that one should not kindle the fires of controversy against one's fellow humans. And, finally, the sabbath offers us a moment of quiet, or serenity, of self-transcendence, a moment that allows us to seek and perhaps achieve some kind of internal peace.

That sounds *exactly* like what our world needs now. It is exactly what I need right now—to stop arguing and pushing and wrestling—for one day a week! Entering into this God-ordained rhythm is one very concrete way in which God's people can become partakers of the divine nature (2 Peter 1:4). Sabbath is a means of grace, a practice that creates channels for God to impart something of God's self so *we* can then be a conduit of God's nature to the world.

When we first start practicing the sabbath, we might not always experience this peace and serenity right away or even every time. The first thing we might experience is the discomfort of discovering how addicted we are to human striving and hard work; we might discover that we do not even know who we are when we are not working. As we unplug from our normal ways of being connected, we might experience intensifying feelings of angst or fear of missing out, or we might be ambushed by emotions we have kept at bay by staying so distracted and busy. This is all very normal and most of us will encounter some of these inner dynamics from time to time, making sabbath feel anything but peaceful. But after twenty years of practice and learning to wait through the initial discomfort, my experience now is that this peace, this tranquility, this shalom descends more quickly as I unplug and power down, trusting my weary soul to God. Given the stresses and strains that are part and parcel of life in a fallen world, what God does in and through my feeble attempts to try and enter in is a wonder each and every time.

SABBATH AS CEASING

Pastor David Alves offers this important clarification about what God actually did on the seventh day that is very helpful for our own reflection:

The Hebrew word shabbat, used by God in Genesis, is really a *stopping* or *ceasing* more than a *rest*. God never tires. He did not *rest* on the seventh day. He is the one who never sleeps nor slumbers. He needs no rest. Bible translators would have better served us to stay closer to the denotative definition of the Hebrew than to have made it seem that God just took a short breather. He *ceased* from his work. He *stopped* what he was doing. That is what *He* meant to communicate. Therefore, that is what he calls *us* to do on *our* Sabbath—make an abrupt end to our labor. All labor? No, our *usual* labor—the labor we've been doing the other six days of the seven-day week.

One of the reasons I find this nuance to be so life-giving is there are some activities that could be considered work that bring such delight to me I actually save them for the sabbath—so I can savor them rather than just push through to check them off my list.

One of those activities is being in my yard planting new plants, adding a few flowers, observing the beauty and the growth of what's already there; wandering around to rejoice at the tiny new shoots of perennials as they emerge from winter, the buds on my flowering trees, the courage of the daffodils as they dazzle us with their color before knowing if winter is even over yet. On the sabbath, I move slowly, dig deeply in the soil, pull up a dandelion here and there, and savor God's good earth without worrying about having a little bit of it under my fingernails. During the different seasons, being present in nature actually puts me in touch *experientially* with the different dynamics that undergird the spiritual life. Wayne Muller writes,

21

Sabbath honors the necessary wisdom of dormancy. If certain plant species, for example, do not lie dormant in the winter, they will not bear fruit in the spring. If this continues for more than a season, the plant begins to die. If dormancy continues to be prevented, the entire species will die. A period of rest—in which nutrition and fertility most readily coalesce—is not simply a human psychological convenience; it is a spiritual and biological necessity. A lack of dormancy produces confusion and erosion in the life force.

Where else can we actually learn this except by being in the garden? Yes, I suppose you could call this work, but it is a different kind of work, done in a different way. On the sabbath, I settle more deeply into the soil of my own life and call it good. And not just good, but very good! Now, if farming or gardening is your everyday work, this might be a different kind of choice for you and it probably should be! But the point here seems to be an emphasis on ceasing one's *usual* labors, whatever that is for each one of us. Tilden Edwards speaks to this distinction when he writes,

> The principle involved here . . . is not so much the physical nature of the activity but its *purpose*. If its intent signifies human power over nature, if it shows human mastery of the world by the purposeful and constructive exercise of intelligence and skill, then it is *meluchah*, work, that violates the restful intent of Sabbath time to recognize our dependence on God as ultimate Creator-Sustainer.

What is so important about this clarification is that it keeps us all on the hook—in the best possible way. No one can say (like I did for the first half of my adult life), "I'm not tired so I don't need a sabbath," or "I'm so busy and my work is so important that I can't afford to take a sabbath." The fact that the God of the universe, who is infinite in time, space, and energy, chose to cease usual labor on the seventh day—not because of exhaustion but because the rhythm itself is simply good—offers a beacon of hope for us all. It is a manifestation of God's innate goodness that is oh-so good for us.

THE BEAUTY IS IN THE RHYTHM

But let's be careful not to create any false dualisms here. What the creation narrative clearly shows us is that the beauty of all this is in the rhythm. Work is not better than rest nor is rest better than work; God did both, and the goodness is in the movement back and forth between the two.

Work offers us the privilege of partnering with God in God's creative purposes through the use of our gifts and our own life-giving energies. It can be a place of deep union and communion with God if we know how to approach it with that desire and intent. As Fr. Ron Rolheiser states so beautifully,

> We know God not just in our conscious awareness and in prayer, but also in a deep inchoate way, by participating with Him in building this world—by growing things, building things, carving things, creating things, cleaning things, painting things, writing things, raising children, nursing bodies, teaching others, consoling others, humoring others, struggling with others, and loving others. Work, like prayer, is a privileged way to get to know God because, when we work, we are toiling in partnership with Him.

And thanks be to God for that, since most of us spend eight to ten hours at work each day!

In a very real sense, work gives meaning to our rest because without work, there would be no reason to rest. But rest also gives meaning to our work as we step back from it, behold it, take the time to call it good, and savor its fruits.

When we practice ceasing in the way God intends, we touch the very ground of our being. We experience ourselves to be creatures in the presence of our Creator—beloved children who are cared for and loved as human beings rather than as human doings. We begin to actually *feel* the love our heavenly Parent has for us beyond what we can produce or accomplish, which is part of the tenderness of the day—at least this is what happens to me. To experience ourselves cherished for *who we are* while not achieving anything or doing anything to earn the air we breathe is a revelation each and every sabbath. As we allow our energies to be replenished—rather than behaving like automatons who can just keep going and going—we are able to reengage our work as energized partners with God in the goodness God wants to bring about in the world.

Wayne Muller offers another metaphor that helps us grasp the beauty of this rhythm.

In the book of Exodus we read "In six days God made heaven and earth, and on the seventh day God rested and was refreshed." Here, the word "refreshed," *vaiynafesh,* literally means, *and God exhaled.* The creation of the world was like a life-quickening inhale; the Sabbath is the exhale. Thus, in the beginning, all creation moves with the rhythm of the inhale and the exhale. Without the sabbath exhale, the life-giving inhale is impossible.

THE GOAL OF ALL EXISTENCE

The weekly rhythm of work and rest here on this earth is a powerful end in itself *and* it points to a far greater reality. For the Israelites, their weekly sabbath pointed to the greater reality that they would eventually "rest" from the rigors of their wilderness journey by entering into the Promised Land where they would finally settle and live on God's terms for them. Today, the weekly sabbath practiced by God's people points to the greater reality of the ultimate rest God is preparing for us in heaven. The writer of Hebrews connects the dots between the Israelites' experience of struggle to enter into God's rest and our own struggle—in chapters three and four the practice of sabbath rest presently and the promise of eternal rest are inextricably intertwined:

> Therefore, while the promise of entering his rest is still open, let us take care that none of you should seem to have failed to reach it. . . . A sabbath rest still remains for the people of God; for those who enter God's rest also cease from their labors as God did from his. Let us therefore make every effort to enter that rest, so that no one may fall through such disobedience as theirs. (Hebrews 4:1, 9-11)

Clearly the issue of rest is really important to God; in a paradoxical way, sabbath keeps us present in the here and now while at the same time pointing to the hope of eternal shalom in the future. As it turns out, sabbath rest is not an optional reprieve in the midst of an otherwise frantic or obsessive life. It is the goal of all existence.

What Your Soul Wants to Say to God

Give yourself a few moments to reflect on the truth that sabbath begins with God, that it is a part of God's very nature, that God then shares with creation by embedding this pattern within it. What does this mean to you, or what could it mean if you let it fully sink in?

Hebrews 4:1-11 contains a rather stirring ode to the promise of rest that still remains open for us as the people of God. The writer encourages us to make every effort to enter into that rest so that no one may fall through disobedience and hardness of heart. Read this passage slowly and reflectively, allowing yourself to wonder if there is any way in which you have hardened your heart toward God's invitation to rest or if there is any resistance to this promise. It might be practical resistance (I just don't know how I can make it work in my life), psychological (I've worked hard all my life and I really don't know who I am when I'm not working and producing), or spiritual (I'm so used to depending on myself that I'm not sure I really believe God will provide for me if I take a break one day a week); or maybe it's something else. But the point is, take this opportunity to go all the way to the bottom of any resistance you feel, and talk to God about it.

Now reflect on 2 Peter 1:4. Does it resonate with you at all that perhaps sabbath rest is one of God's "precious and very great promises"? What is it like to consider practicing rhythms of work and rest as one way we can become partakers in the divine nature?

3

FINDING FREEDOM
THROUGH RESISTANCE

● ● ●

If you aren't resting, you are a slave to something.

ADELE CALHOUN

IN THEIR BOOK *Everyday Sabbath,* professors Paul Patton
and Robert Woods tell the story of an experience they each had
on a Sunday afternoon, an experience that eventually drew
them to write their book together.

> On that fateful Sunday, shortly after we returned home
> from church in our respective states, each of us grabbed
> some lunch, headed for the recliner, and spent nearly nine
> hours watching three successive football games. When
> the last whistle blew, we turned off the television and sat
> alone in the quiet dark. For some this might sound like an
> ideal day. But as we surveyed the open chip bags and
> candy wrappers, we felt exhausted and depressed. The
> clocks on the wall mocked us. Nine hours of life were gone

forever because we decided there was nothing better to do that afternoon.

Sadly, this was not the first experience of this kind for either of us. . . . As embarrassing as our Sunday afternoon football fiasco is to admit, we are grateful for the wake-up call. Sabbath works as an everyday pattern of resistance that disentangles us from the dominance of spectator passivity.

FREEDOM JOURNEY

We tend to think of sabbath as being mostly about rest and replenishment—and it is!—but if that's all we emphasize, it can come across as being rather soft. For those who were first given the gift of sabbath, it was so much more than that: it was the sign, symbol, and lived reality of their *resistance to* and *liberation from* oppression. To fully understand the meaning of sabbath we must locate it within the Exodus narrative, within the lives of real people in a real time and place who practiced resistance to cultural realities that were enslaving them. As Patton and Woods so powerfully illustrate in their embarrassing little story, we too are enslaved to many aspects of life in our culture and the practice of sabbath *illuminates* our path to freedom. If we look a little closer at the sabbath in its original context we might notice that it is really a tale of resistance.

When instructions were first given for sabbath-keeping in Exodus 16, God was communicating in the strongest possible terms that God's people were now free—free from all aspects of their bondage to the Egyptians. For many years the Israelites had been captive to Pharaoh's system of endless production that was legitimized by the gods Pharaoh worshiped. It was a secure existence but they had no personal freedom, and especially not the freedom to take a day of rest. Pharaoh, who was nothing more than a hard-nosed production manager, kept increasing their quotas in order to amass his own wealth; Exodus 5 is a brutal description of a relentless production schedule in which rest was impossible and disallowed.

As slaves in Egypt, the people of Israel were always at the mercy of the demands and expectations of a relentlessly consumeristic and opportunistic ruler who cared nothing for their well-being. But now . . . now that they had been freed from their bondage, they were being guided into a way of life that *worked for them*, by a God who knew them and loved them and only wanted to give them the very best. Walter Brueggemann writes,

> Into this system of hopeless weariness erupts the God of the burning bush (Exodus 3:1-6). *That* God heard the despairing fatigue of the slaves (2:23-25), resolved to liberate the slave company of Israel from that exploitive system (3:7-9), and recruited Moses for the human task of emancipation (3:10). The reason Miriam and the other women can sing and dance at the end of the exodus narrative is the emergence of a new social reality in which the life of the Israelite economy is no longer determined and compelled by the insatiable production quotas of Egypt and its gods (15:20-21).

It should not escape our notice that when the Ten Commandments (including the sabbath) are introduced for the first time, God begins by saying, "I am the Lord your God who brought you out of the land of Egypt, out of the house of slavery" (Exodus 20:1-2). There are many other ways their Deliverer could have been identified, but in choosing this emphasis the

Israelites are reminded of a core piece of the Holy One's identity—that of a liberating God who freed them from bondage to Pharaoh and to a system that only valued them according to what they could produce. God is connecting the dots between the experience of being delivered from oppression and the principles and practices that will undergird a whole new way of life; after all, those who are used to living in bondage do not know how to live as free people until someone shows them. The very same God who was free to rest from work on the seventh day would now be known as *the God who emancipates* God's people from bondage to a system that enslaved them. No wonder Walter Brueggemann states that "the fourth commandment is the most difficult and the most urgent of the commandments in our society . . . because it defies the most elemental requirements of a commodity-propelled society specializing in control and entertainment, bread and circuses . . . along with anxiety and violence."

Considered in this light, there is nothing "soft" about sabbath. By instituting the sabbath, God intervened in human history to make right something that had gone terribly wrong and re-established a pattern present in creation that had been tragically lost. In the Exodus narrative, the God who is free to rest on the seventh day is calling the people God loves to *participate* in his freedom by embedding it in their national identity.

PATTERNS OF RESISTANCE

Does anything about this reflection on Israel's enslavement remind you of the bondage many of us are experiencing today within our current culture—bondage to patterns of relentless productivity, never-enough consumerism, the constant stimulation of push notifications and connectivity that exacerbates stress, anxiety, and bitter controversies? Is there anything about the description of God as one who emancipates and frees people from their bondage that offers hope that we could be freed from our bondage as well?

When we think of sabbath only in terms of rest and replenishment, we are selling it short. In Jewish tradition, sabbath contains a strong element of resistance to the prevailing culture, and to the gods within that culture, as allegiance is proclaimed to the God who is our God. The practice of sabbath-keeping was and is an act of resistance against a culture that brainwashes us into thinking that good things come only through unceasing determination, tireless human effort, and always being plugged in. And it's not just an act of resistance against forces that are external. Our practice deepens as we recognize and resist the *internal* drivenness, self-determination, and individualism that has been planted and cultivated in us. Our resistance is solidified as, one day a week, we take ourselves out of the soupy mess this potent combination has us swimming in.

One day a week we practice trusting in God as our ultimate strength and provider rather than putting all our faith in what we can secure for ourselves through our 24-7 striving. We practice humility and dependence on God as we settle into the limits of our humanity and rest one day a week. Remembering how we used to live and how God has freed us from our bondage leads quite naturally to delight and devotion as we determine once again that we will not get sucked back into a life of nonfreedom. Sabbath is first and foremost about the freedom to live our lives on God's terms for us rather than living in bondage to anyone, anything, or any culture. It is about the God who is free to cease laboring and to rest, marking out a path for us to live in freedom as well.

And sabbath is not just for the privileged few. In its original context, sabbath was intended to be the great equalizer, ensuring that all God's creatures—including the animals!—would receive the benefits of this life-enhancing pattern.

> Six days you shall labor and do all your work. But the seventh day is a sabbath to the LORD your God; you shall not do any work—you, or your son or daughter, or your male or female slave, or your ox or your donkey, or any of your livestock, or the resident alien in your towns, so that your male and female slave may rest as well as you. (Deuteronomy 5:13-14)

The reference to slavery is uncomfortable in light of current sensibilities, but let's not miss the point—that regardless of gender, family position, socioeconomic status, citizenship, or even animal species, sabbath is for all God's creatures. Kelly Kapic writes,

> One of the most countercultural and radical ideas in the Bible, when compared with the ancient world, is the sabbath. One day a week you do not have to work [and] the Jews were thought lazy because of it. While those in power could rest when they wanted, slaves and peasants were often unprotected from the demands for endless labor, a terrible burden still on the poor of our day who have multiple jobs to make ends meet or are trapped in other modern forms of slavery.

One concern we might have about sabbath-keeping is that it smacks of privilege, an impossibility for those living in poverty, working multiple jobs, or perhaps "hustling" low-paying jobs to make ends meet. It is important to realize that this is an issue created by our current culture, not one created by the practice itself as God gave it. Some of us have been alive long enough to remember a time when Sundays were different from the other days, and as a culture we upheld a form of sabbath: commerce ceased, most businesses were closed, and sports teams did not compete. Whether you were religious or not, cultural practices generally supported this rhythm for everyone. We are far from that reality today and there is great loss of support for this practice. Objections about sabbath as an expression of privilege emphasize current cultural realities over the very essence of sabbath as God has given it—as though cultural realities are more significant than God's intentions. In some ways it doesn't really matter that today sabbath feels like privilege, as though the way it *feels* to us makes it so. As Dorothy Bass states so compellingly, "When we keep a Sabbath holy, we are practicing, for a day, the freedom God intends for all people."

Norman Wirzba, a professor at Duke Divinity school who pursues research and teaching at the intersections of theology, philosophy, ecology, agriculture, and environmental studies, goes even further. He articulates the idea of a *sabbath economy* in the spirit of our God who executes justice for the oppressed, gives food to the hungry, sets prisoners free, and lifts up the bowed down (Psalm 146:7-9). He defines a sabbath economy as one that will have *the equitable distribution of resources* as a foremost goal. As the ancient Israelite model makes clear, "equitable distribution" does not mean that all people must enjoy the same or the same amount of goods. Uniformity is not the goal. What is crucial is that we be attentive to when we have enough and fully alert to when others do not have basic needs met. Just as the Israelites were aware that land (wealth) accumulation meant that others were pushed into states of deprivation and want, so we too must guard against the kinds of inequities that further diminish the capacities of others to live well.

We might not know exactly how to bring about this kind of equality in our current culture, but that does not change the fact that in God's economy sabbath is the great equalizer—the great leveler—and it is our job to figure out how to make it so today. A faithful sabbath practice actually calls us to it.

A TIME TO REMEMBER

In the book of Deuteronomy, Moses gives a retrospective on his life in leadership and reflects on the Israelite journey and that pivotal moment when God gave them the Ten Commandments. With the benefit of hindsight, he contextualizes the sabbath even more firmly within this theme of liberation and radical equality. "Remember that you were a slave in the land of Egypt, and the LORD your God brought you out from there with a mighty hand and an outstretched arm; *therefore,* the LORD your God commanded you to keep the sabbath day" (Deuteronomy 5:6, 15, emphasis added). Taking our cues from Moses, we see that one of the main functions of sabbath-keeping is to give us a regular, built-in opportunity for remembering who we are and to whom we belong. No matter how enslaved we've been during the week, on the sabbath we remember our true identity as free people. We remember how God has been with us, liberating us in the first place, and we find our freedom once again so we can continue to live on God's terms for us. Cole Arthur Riley, the creator of Black Liturgies, says,

> When we rest, we do so in memory of rest denied. We receive what has been withheld from ourselves and our ancestors. And our present respite draws us into remembrance of those who were not permitted it. . . . When I rest my eyes, I meet those ancestors and they meet me, as time blurs within us. They tell me to sit back. They tell me to breathe. They tell me to walk away like they couldn't. Rest is an act of defiance. . . . It's the audacity to face the demands of this world and proclaim, *We will not be owned.*

To practice sabbath, we need to know what we are in bondage to, what has us in its grip, and that is precisely the thing we should cease. We need to know what wears us out and what wears us down—what robs us of our joy and peace—and cease *that,* because that is exactly what God wants to free us from. That said, I conclude this chapter with my own embarrassing admission.

Early on in the Covid-19 pandemic I started watching the news every night to see reports on the numbers—positivity rates, hospitalizations, deaths, updates on mask mandates and vaccines. I have never been one to watch the news regularly, but not knowing where in the news hour the Covid-19 numbers would be reported, it was easy to get hooked waiting for this piece of news, and before long an hour (or even two!) would have gone by. Since we were all sheltering at home there really wasn't much else to do, so it didn't seem like that big of a deal at first. Add to this the drama, unpredictability, and divisiveness of the political scene and it was easy to spend entire evenings careening down rabbit holes that left me sad, mad, depressed, and confounded about what was happening in our country. To make matters worse, my husband and I tend to approach news and politics from very different points of view and watching the news together often put us on edge with each other—not good.

Ordering my life around watching the news was such a new development that it took me a while to realize what was happening. Once I realized how much time I was frittering away and how my increased attention to the news was affecting my soul, I identified this as a place of bondage in my life, an addiction, which by definition was something I couldn't stop doing even though I knew it wasn't good for me. Fortunately, because I had been practicing sabbath for so long, I recognized that a more disciplined sabbath practice was my path to freedom from this very stressful aspect of life. I determined not to watch the news from the beginning of sabbath on Saturday nights through the end of sabbath on Sundays.

It's not that watching the news is inherently bad; it was my addiction that made it bad *for me*.

Of course, there are times I am still tempted and sometimes I give in; but once I started living into this particular sabbath discipline, if felt like a relief to know I wouldn't be subjecting myself to the twenty-four-hour news cycle on a day when I was supposed to be experiencing peace and serenity. And eventually I experienced greater freedom to make better choices other days of the week as well.

RESTORED TO OUR TRUE IDENTITY

Many of us have fallen into the trap of identifying ourselves by what we *do*, but sabbath cultivates a sense of identity around who we fundamentally *are*. Richard Rohr points out, "We have no real access to who we really are except in God. Only when we rest in God can we find the safety, the spaciousness, and the scary freedom to be who we are, all that we are, more than we are, and less than we are."

Sabbath is an opportunity to find ourselves in God again. Sabbath restores us to a sense of our truest identity as God speaks into our souls and whispers to each and every one of us: *Remember. Remember who you are—you are precious in my sight and I love you. Remember who I am and that you belong to me—I have redeemed you for my purposes; I have called you by name. You are mine. Remember what I have done for you in liberating you from your bondage and remember that I have the power do it again. I can and I will; and, in fact, I am already doing it.*

What Your Soul Wants to Say to God

There are some really packed phrases in this chapter—phrases that are packed with theological substance and spiritual significance. Which phrases reached out and grabbed you or caused some other kind of visceral response? Underline them or copy them into your journal, allowing yourself to react and respond to them.

How do you respond to the idea of sabbath as resistance to cultural bondage and to our own internal drivenness and hopeless weariness?

At the end of this chapter, I shared an example of becoming aware of an area of bondage in my own life. Is there any area where you are aware that you are in bondage to some kind of addiction—addiction to performance and success, productivity, approval, making money, gathering information, being right—anything that has you in its grip that prevents you from ceasing and resting? How can sabbath provide needed structure for ceasing in order to experience the freedom God offers? Write in your journal about this.

Talk with a spiritual friend or spiritual director about your sense of being in bondage in this way and how much you long for freedom. What would it look like to practice sabbath as a way of resisting bondage in order to say yes to a deeper kind of freedom?

4

DISCOVERING SABBATH
in COMMUNITY

● ● ●

The LORD said to Moses: You yourself are to speak to
the Israelites: "You shall keep my sabbaths."

EXODUS 31:12-13

JOHN BUCHANAN, A PRESBYTERIAN MINISTER and
long-time editor and publisher of the *Christian Century*, tells
this delightfully earthy tale about his early education in
sabbath-keeping. He writes:

> My instructor in Sabbath-keeping was not a professor or
> spiritual director, but a foreman at the East Chicago
> Inland Steel plant named Mike Paddock. His wife was the
> treasurer of the tiny congregation I served as a student
> pastor, and she wrote my salary check twice a month.
> Mike would deliver it along with two dozen eggs and a
> shopping bag full of tomatoes, cucumbers and honey dew
> melons. Mike's seminar on Sabbath-keeping occurred on

a summer Saturday morning when he saw my car at the church.

"What the hell are you doing here on a Saturday morning?" he asked me.

"Well," I stammered, "I'm here being available to the congregation. I'm pretty much gone all week, at school, so Saturday I'm here in case anybody needs me."

"Let me tell you something," Mike said. "Nobody needs you today. If they do, they'll call you. Nobody wants to see you today. They're busy. They'll see plenty of you tomorrow. So go home. Cut your grass, wash your car, sit in your yard, play with your kids. Get outa' here."

I did what he said and have tried to abide by it ever since.

Would that we all had such excellent teaching on the finer nuances of sabbath-keeping within our communities!

THE GIFT WE DON'T KNOW HOW TO RECEIVE

When I think about the sabbath these days, I am struck by a couple of things. First of all, I am struck by the fact that sabbath is a gift from God that so few of us have figured out how to open. It's a bit like leaving a beautifully wrapped present in the middle of your living room for years because you'd rather look at it and talk about how beautiful the wrapping is than find out what's inside.

My dad used to do this on Christmas morning and drive us all crazy. He would slow down the proceedings considerably, taking an inordinate amount of time to admire the wrapping paper and bow, saying he wished he didn't have to open it because the wrapping was so beautiful. He would put off opening the gift for as long as possible, and then when he did open it, he was so slow, painstakingly trying not to rip the paper! We tolerated all this for about three seconds—appreciating his appreciation of good wrapping—but eventually all manner of pressure had to be brought to get him to open the present because we, as the givers, were most excited for him to see what was inside.

I wonder if God feels the same way as God waits for us to actually open the gift of sabbath rather than just sit around talking about it.

I am also struck by how many individuals and families are trying to figure out sabbath all by themselves when, in fact, sabbath-keeping is a *communal* discipline that needs to be led and practiced in community. These days it seems like people who long for sabbath are left to their own devices because churches and ministries are not leading out on it; in fact, churches' schedules and priorities often seem to work against the very practice God gave for our good.

I will never forget the disappointment I felt when, during a season of simply attending church (rather than being on staff), I made the disturbing discovery that it wasn't so much the secular culture that prevented our family from keeping a sabbath as much as it was *the church*! Of course there was the normal stress and strain of getting everyone up, dressed, fed, and out the door for Sunday morning services—which doesn't always feel restful—but then when we started to get involved, we discovered that the rest of the day was filled with youth group activities, committee meetings, choir practices, small groups, and congregational gatherings. Sometimes those included voting, decision-making, and announcing hard news that could shatter even the most spiritual person's sense of peace and rest!

I expected Sunday to be a workday while I was on staff at a church; but when the opportunity to be a "normal" family and just attend church for a while resulted in our family barely being able to find two hours to share a meal together—let alone settle into a different way of being for a whole day—I was deeply disillusioned. I had to face the fact that it wasn't the secular culture that made it all seem so impossible—it was the Christian busyness that has come to characterize contemporary church life.

WHAT ARE WE INVITING PEOPLE TO?

This brings me to a question that is crucial for us as Christian leaders today: When we invite people to join us in Christian community, what are we really inviting them into? A life of Christian busyness or a way of life that works? These days joining a church seems to be fairly synonymous with signing up for a life of Christian busyness layered onto lives that already feel unmanageable. Is it any wonder that so many younger Christians—the "nones and the dones"—are responding with, "Thanks, but no thanks!"? The "dones" have already been there and done that. The "nones" can't figure out why anyone would try it in the first place!

At the same time, there is also a group of serious and deeply spiritual young adults (many with young families) who are sincerely looking for churches that will teach, guide, and support them in this countercultural rhythm, but such communities seem to be nonexistent. The communal nature of sabbath-keeping is one aspect of this life-giving practice that is most missing in contemporary literature and in my own explorations. We lack a clear call to the communal nature of sabbath-keeping, which means we are lacking the leadership needed for whole communities to embrace sabbath-keeping together. Yet, our ability to practice sabbath effectively relies on this communal element.

I have also wondered if there is a subtle misconception at work that needs to be cleared up in order for us to embrace sabbath. *Sabbath is not the same thing as solitude and silence.* By definition, solitude and silence are practices we enter into with God and God alone. Sabbath, by definition, is a practice we enter into with others, in community. Although one may be able to incorporate solitude and silence into their sabbath practice (and we certainly should if we can), generally speaking sabbath is meant to be discovered in community; it is not something for individuals to stumble around and try to figure out for themselves, by themselves. It is a practice to be taught, led, and supported corporately so everyone can embrace it together.

When God first instituted the sabbath it was in the context of community, given to the community through their leader. It was in community that they learned how to order their lives around shared rhythms that would shape them individually and together. Let's face it—when the sabbath life is not embraced intentionally by the whole community, the decisions and patterns lived out in our communities can actually work *against* individuals' best intentions, no matter what we are preaching from the pulpit. And when these patterns work against any meaningful practice of sabbath-keeping—so pivotal for a life well-lived in God—it can cause people to question whether to remain or whether to search out a community that can support them in finding sane rhythms of work and rest.

PRACTICING TRUST

Sabbath-keeping, and the deeper truths it represents, is a vibrant thread that begins with God in creation, is woven into the lives of God's people immediately following their emancipation, and is then carried through the New Testament. For the Israelites, sabbath-keeping was so important to their new way of life that God's instructions about it actually preceded the Ten Commandments. In Exodus 16, when the Israelites began experiencing how risky their situation was, they complained against Moses and Aaron, pining for the security of life in Egypt "when we sat by the fleshpots and ate our fill of bread." They even accused Moses and Aaron of intentionally bringing them out to the wilderness to die (Exodus 16:1-3). Clearly this was not their best moment. And it was at this fragile juncture in their journey that God intervened and established a daily pattern of providing quail and manna, along with the clear instruction that they were to gather only as much as their household needed for one day. "Morning by morning they gathered it, as much as each needed; but when the sun grew hot, it melted" (Exodus 16:21). Then on the sixth day, God led them into an even deeper level of trust by instructing them to gather enough food for two days so they could cease and rest on the seventh, patterning themselves after God's rhythm in creation.

In its earliest iteration, sabbath was about learning to trust God's provision, and the people's capacity to follow God in this rhythm was actually a test of their obedience. Moses' role was key in this whole process. As their anointed leader, he was the mouthpiece for God and it was his responsibility to give them very practical and specific guidance for how to observe this important day.

> This is what the LORD has commanded: "Tomorrow is a day of solemn rest, a holy sabbath to the LORD; bake what you want to bake and boil what you want to boil, and all that is left put aside to be kept until morning." So they put it aside until morning, as Moses commanded them; and it did not become foul and there were not worms in it. Moses said, "Eat it today, for today is a sabbath to the LORD." (Exodus 16:23-25)

To fully understand the practice of sabbath-keeping, we must see it as integrally connected with trust—an increasing capacity to trust God for provision in the life of God's people (Exodus 16:9-12). To miss this is to miss one of the main points.

At first the people of Israel were simply unable to trust God's provision and do it God's way. Even with such specific instructions, they messed up on their first try. But as their shepherd and leader, Moses stayed right with them, continuing to interpret and reiterate the significance of this important element of their shared life. Although Moses might have felt he had better things to do than to teach these slow learners about the sabbath, he stuck with it after God repeated the instruction: "'See! The LORD has given you the sabbath, therefore on the sixth day he gives you food for two days; each of you stay where you are; do not leave your place on the seventh day.' So the people rested on the seventh day" (Exodus 16:29-30).

Little by little, under Moses' guidance, the people learned how to order their lives around a shared practice that helped them cease their labors and trust God's provision. Through this very concrete discipline, they lived out their faith that what they accomplished in six days would be enough, and on the seventh day they could take their hand off the plow, trusting God to keep running the world without them. Over time, the daily rhythm (of gathering only as much manna as they needed each day) and the weekly rhythm (of gathering enough on the sixth day to carry over to the seventh) shaped their identity as individual souls and also as a people journeying together in God's presence. Later on, sabbath-keeping would be included in the Ten Commandments, but first it was simply God's guidance into a way of life that was good for them, signaling that their lives were changing for the better under a loving God.

After God gave Moses the Ten Commandments and many other instructions, and right before Moses came down from the mountain, God reiterated his instruction to Moses and emphasized his leadership in this important area by saying, "You yourself are to speak to the Israelites [and say]: 'You shall keep my sabbaths'" (Exodus 31:13). Clearly, there was no delegating this one. Sabbath-keeping was so radical and subversive it needed to be taught, modeled, and led by the person in the community who had the most spiritual authority. *Sabbath-keeping needed to be led*, intentionally and consistently, by a leader who was learning his own hard lessons about sustainable living.

THE MAKING OF A SABBATH LEADER

God is always out ahead of us, preparing what we need before we even know we need it. This was certainly true for the

Israelites. Before they even realized the extent of their bondage, before their taskmasters had made their lives more miserable by increasing their quotas and telling them they had to make bricks without straw, before they realized how bad it was going to get . . . God was way out ahead of them preparing a leader to show them the way out. Through a significant moral failure followed by a season of devasting self-awareness, profound hiddenness, and a wild encounter with a burning bush, God was equipping Moses to be a leader who would risk everything to champion their freedom. And it was that leader, the one who had won their respect by leading them out of Egypt, who was charged with guiding them into sabbath-keeping—not merely as sign and symbol of their newfound freedom, but as the *lived reality* of freedom itself.

It's no coincidence that during the very same time period in which the people of Israel were learning about sabbath, Moses was being humbled by his own limitations through his father-in-law Jethro's keen observation that his schedule and his workload were unmanageable. Even though it is usually best for fathers-in-law to stay out of such things, Jethro got right in Moses' face and said: "What you are doing is not good. You will surely wear yourself out, both you and these people with you. For the task is too heavy for you" (Exodus 18:17-18). (Given the fact that Jethro had been taking care of Moses' wife and children because Moses' lifestyle was not conducive to having his family with him, Jethro probably felt he was well within his rights to comment.)

Amazingly, Moses submitted to the wisdom of this spiritual leader/priest who was older and more experienced, and he submitted to life in community *with* others and *for* others. Jethro

47

was clear that this guidance was not given merely for Moses' personal benefit—as important as that was—it was given for the good of his whole community. Even though Moses felt he was indispensable (Exodus 18:15-16), Jethro was telling him that his community needed him to bring his best, rested, alert self to his leadership, not his exhausted, burned out, driven self. So after giving good, concrete advice about sharing leadership so as to lighten his load, Jethro puts an even finer point on the importance of this for the community by saying, "If you do this, . . . then you will be able to endure, and all these people will go to their home in peace" (Exodus 18:23). What seemed to be very intimate guidance for Moses' personal well-being was actually for the sake of others in the community God had given him to lead.

In response to Jethro's wisdom and his very practical suggestions about sharing the leadership load with others, Moses identified other discerning leaders to carry the burden with him so that he could, indeed, engage in a more sustainable lifestyle. In this way, his teachings and instructions on sabbath were more than just repeating God's commands; they came from his own struggle to find a way of life that worked on all levels, and that became his platform.

INNER AUTHORITY

Sabbath-keeping and other aspects of self-care are not merely self-indulgent luxuries; they are part and parcel of healthy leadership that is sustainable for the long haul. It is what gives an authentic platform from which to teach and guide others. In order for communities to order their lives around sane rhythms of work and rest, it is essential for respected leaders to live within a sustainable lifestyle themselves and to champion sabbath-keeping as a spiritual practice as significant as Scripture reading, prayer, and confession. These are leaders who have tried and failed and grown in their capacity to cultivate sane rhythms of work and rest. From their own personal experience, they understand the pitfalls and temptations of attempting something as radical as sabbath-keeping, yet through focus and concerted effort they have made the sabbath the centerpiece of their life in the midst of a culture that knows nothing of the freedom God offers.

Thus, when they speak and invite others into this way of life, they do so with an inner authority that comes from having tasted the blessedness of it. They are not strident or pushy because they don't need to be; their winsome way is inviting to all who are in touch with their humanness. Of course, they teach (and they must!), but the weight of their authority comes from being grounded in the goodness of this practice as they have experienced it in their own life.

If the Israelite experience teaches us anything, it is that sabbath-keeping was always meant to be a communal practice and not merely a privatized one. And it all starts with leadership.

What Your Soul Wants to Say to God

Take a moment to sit quietly with the truths presented in this chapter—sabbath as a communal discipline and the role of leadership in cultivating such a community. How do you respond to the idea that teaching and guiding your community into sabbath-keeping and structuring your communal life around it is one aspect of your responsibility as a leader? Do you feel resonance or resistance? Burdened or hopeful? Do not focus yet on how you might implement all of this. For now just notice your honest response and speak to God about it.

Reflect on your own personal journey with the sabbath. Do you have a sabbath practice? If so, how are you experiencing it these days? What would a spiritual mentor observe in your life—anything like what Jethro observed about Moses? Do you have an older, wiser leader with whom you can speak honestly about your way of life?

If you were to lead your community in a sabbath way of life, would your patterns and practices give you the inner authority to lead authentically? In the following chapters we will take next steps in establishing, reviewing, or refining our own sabbath practice.

5

THE POWER
of UNPLUGGING

● ● ●

Nothing is better for your computer or your body than
a complete shutdown and restart. Each. Week.

TIFFANY SHLAIN

WHEN I FIRST STARTED practicing sabbath over twenty years ago, the biggest challenge was turning off my computer, staying out of my home office, and truly saying no to my work. Work was the addiction I was most aware of and all my focus was on trying to say no to the hold that work, productivity, and achievement had on me. I remember processing the challenge this posed to my sabbath-keeping with a spiritual friend, and she suggested that I take the life-size statue of St. Francis I have in my office and move it in front of my office door as a guard and a sentinel to keep me out of my workspace on Sundays!

But today I am aware of struggling with a different issue, and that is my addiction to technology and how hard it is to disconnect from my phone for any length of time at all, let alone for a whole day. When I first started practicing sabbath, there were no smartphones. There were cellphones, but they weren't "smart"; they existed to make phone calls and that was about it. We all still had landlines and that was the primary way families stayed in touch, people were reached in an emergency, and vendors and doctor's offices confirmed or changed appointments.

All of that is hard to imagine now because it is so far in the rearview mirror. Most of us have gotten rid of our landlines so the only way to connect with family and friends is on our mobile phones. Scheduling and confirming important appointments is now accomplished, for the most part, through automated notification by text. Now most people do not even go to the bathroom, go for a walk, or go to bed without their phone within arm's reach. Most people use their phone to tell time, wake up in the morning, check email, get the news, find out the weather, get directions, report on how well they slept or how many steps they took, and keep track of friends and loved ones on social media. And that is not to mention the ever-present temptation to fill up every spare moment with listening to podcasts and scrolling social media apps, news feeds, and text messages.

The problem, of course, is that keeping our phones with us or strapped to our bodies so we don't miss anything "important" means we are plugged in all the time, open to all manner of interruptions that come any time of the day or night, whether we have asked for them or not.

A NEW KIND OF BONDAGE

Every moment of our lives—important or not—is now subject to intrusion and interruption. Even when we are with the most precious people in our lives or in the midst of some of the most special moments of our lives, there is something in us obsessively wondering what we might be missing out on. Sherry Turkle, author of *Alone Together*, states in an article in the *New York Times*,

> Our phones are not accessories but psychologically potent devices that change not just what we do but who we are. . . . Studies of conversation both in laboratory and in natural settings show that when two people are talking, the mere presence of a phone on the table between them or in the periphery of their vision changes both what they talk about and the degree of connection they feel. People keep the conversation on topics where they won't mind being interrupted. They don't feel as invested in each other. Even a silent phone disconnects us.

We want to be with each other, but we don't want to miss out on anything going on elsewhere either.

Our whole culture is having trouble with this now, but for those who have any sort of public life at all—pastors, musicians, authors, speakers, bloggers, marketers, salespeople—it's almost impossible to stay present in the moment we're in with the people we're with, grounded in a sense of self, apart from obsessively tracking views, likes, hearts, and comments. The temptation to live our lives completely oriented to these external sources of stimulation is enormous; we are hooked on the jolts of dopamine delivered by likes, hearts, views, and comments, willing to chase the "highs" these brain chemicals create. Even our sense of what makes something real is now connected to whether or not we capture it in filtered photos (unless we designate it #unfiltered, of course!) and make it available for the world to see. The great philosophical question is no longer: "If a tree falls in the forest but no one hears it, did the tree really fall?" It is: "If I saw a sunset, or hosted a cool birthday party for my child, or prepared a gourmet charcuterie board, did it really happen if I did not post it on Instagram?"

Many of us are aware that these technological advances have become a source of the deepest kind of exhaustion, foisted on us in the most manipulative ways by those who do not have our best interests at heart. Whole books have already been written on how these seismic shifts are affecting our minds, our ability to focus, our attention spans, our relationships, and our productivity, not to mention our spirituality and our ability to be quiet and present to the subtle movements of the Spirit in our lives.

I have read deeply and widely on all of this and it concerns me more than I can say, but as Ed Cyzewski says early in his book on digital formation versus spiritual formation,

> We don't necessarily need to wade through research studies or the expert opinions of psychologists to prove that devices and social media apps are designed to become invasive, habit-forming and compulsive—if not a behavioral addiction at times. Many of the people who design digital technology and social media have publicly stated that their products are designed to be toxic, addicting, and manipulative, depriving users of choice and free time through habit-forming feedback loops where the reactions and notifications become the rewards to using social media.

This sounds a whole lot like bondage, doesn't it?

There are many others sounding the alarm about how technology and social media are affecting our humanity (see the section on technology in the bibliography), so I am not going to litigate all of that here. I just hope and pray we are all paying attention. My focus is to state clearly and unequivocally that for all the benefits and efficiencies our technologies afford, being plugged in 24-7 is a major source of exhaustion, overstimulation, discontent, and even personality disorders. One of the most alarming books I've read on this topic is by Dr. Larry Rosen, a research psychologist and computer educator, who has written a book called *iDisorder: Understanding Our Obsession with Technology and Overcoming Its Hold on Us.* In it he puts forth this disturbing premise—that certain technologies seem to be related to specific personality disorders, and that there are critical features embedded in technology that "march us directly to our own personal iDisorder." Then he goes on throughout the book to relentlessly make connections between different kinds of technology and clinical diagnoses like narcissistic personality disorder, obsessive-compulsive disorder, panic and anxiety disorders, media-induced depression and mania, ADHD, and even voyeurism!

Rosen's work and research is so alarming that one can only take in so much at once. I am going to stop here and simply state that the sabbath is our ticket to freedom from a kind of bondage that is so new and unprecedented that we have barely had time to process all the implications. As always, God is out ahead of us, providing a spiritual practice that can deliver us from our enslavement if we can just get in touch with the deeper desires of our hearts—our desire for freedom and rest, presence and delight.

EMBRACING A TECH SHABBAT

In some Jewish families it is customary to have a sabbath box that holds items that will not be needed on the sabbath—equipment associated with work and effort (like tools, phones, computers), really anything that should not be taken into the sacred space of sabbath. Of course, some things would be too big and cumbersome to actually put in the box (for instance, a lawnmower), but Wayne Muller suggests it is possible to put something in the box that would be symbolic of one's work, serving as a reminder of what we are committed to leaving behind as we enter into God's gift of rest. Or we could write on a piece of paper those things that are left undone and may still be weighing on us, along with worries and concerns that we would like to leave behind and/or entrust to God's care.

I have thought about the sabbath box concept a lot over the years, wishing we could all bravely put at least one thing in there—and that is our cellphones (particularly our smartphones) as sign, symbol, and reality of our willingness to unplug completely on this day. In addition to any other items that might symbolize work and stimulation for us, placing our phones in a sabbath box, drawer, or some other out-of-the-way place is to extricate ourselves from the hold our technologies have on us and the way our constant connectedness keeps us from getting any real psychic rest. There are many symptoms and sources of exhaustion for leaders these days, but one of the deepest and most pernicious is the constant stimulation that comes from always being plugged in, stirred up, and constantly promoting ourselves.

A recent study showed that just having your phone nearby—even if it is off—makes you less attentive. I have been noticing this but in an odd sort of way, I find it helpful to have it confirmed by research rather than just continuing to think I might be going crazy because of how the presence of cellphones—on the table, on our wrists, and at the bedside—affect me. I have noticed that when I am with a friend or family member and the phone is on the table but face down, I am less likely to deepen the conversation for fear of being interrupted. Even when the phone is out of sight but on, I am still alert to its vibration and might even imagine that it is vibrating, so I still have to go check. And when someone checks their phone in the middle of a meeting or conversation, it creates an almost reflexive urge to check my own phone as well—if they feel they are missing out on something more important while they are with me, maybe I'm missing out on something more important while I am with them! And don't even get me started on leaving ourselves open to all manner of intrusion to relaxation and sleep by keeping our phones by our beds!

On the other hand (and thank God there is another hand), I have also noticed that when I can manage to unplug completely—for a walk, lunch with a friend, an uninterrupted evening with my spouse, a nap on the couch, a day of solitude and silence, even a whole vacation—I experience an entirely different kind of freedom: an incredible lightness of being in which my soul is buoyed up and renewed like nothing else. It has taken me awhile to observe this enough to believe it is true. And I have decided to honor this knowing by seeking ways to unplug completely from my phone (or at least limit it) on the sabbath for the purpose of finding the deepest kind of rest. I encourage you to do the same.

This is not easy and there are a lot of complicating factors—some very personal to our life situation—but with desire, forethought, and planning, I believe we can do it. Tiffany Shlain's work *24/6: The Power of Unplugging One Day a Week* is tremendously practical and supportive in all of this. An internet pioneer and filmmaker (ironic, isn't it?) who also happens to be a nonreligious Jew, she describes the benefits of what she calls "technology shabbat" in this way:

> Living 24/6 feels like magic and here's why: it seems to defy the laws of physics, as it both slows down time and gives us more of it. I laugh a lot more on that day without screens. I notice everything in greater detail. I sleep better. It strengthens my relationships and makes me feel healthier. It allows me to read, think, be more creative, and reflect in a deeper way. Each week I get a full reset. Afterwards, I am much more productive and efficient, with positive effects that radiate out to the other six days . . . who would have thought technology could be more potent in its absence?

Shlain's book is full of practical ideas for how to maintain a tech shabbat—everything from preparing friends and family that you will be out of the loop, to reinstalling your landline so you can be reached in an emergency, to printing out phone numbers, directions, and other key information you might need for the day. If you are going to include others in your sabbath by inviting them to join you for a meal or activity, she suggests nailing down the details ahead of your sabbath so you don't have to text back and forth on the day of, perhaps even kicking off your sabbath with a beautiful dinner with family and/or friends that signals the beginning of this special twenty-four hours. It takes planning, but to hear her describe it, it is utterly worth it.

Unplugging completely from screens and technology (except, perhaps, for a predetermined movie) is a new layer of sabbath practice I am exploring; it is already making a difference in my ability to enter into a deeper psychic rest for my mind and my emotions and even my nervous system that needs a break from hard news and unnecessary stimulation.

SPEED OF THE LEADER

It is nearly impossible to live sabbath rhythms well and consistently if the communities we are a part of don't support them and if they are not led intentionally from the top down, or "from the center out." For anyone else to feel free to unplug, the leader needs to model the freedom to unplug—which is hard when we feel so responsible for everything and everybody. The pastoral role, in particular, lends itself to feeling like we cannot unplug, because what if someone is on their deathbed, is in a car accident, or experiences some other kind of emergency where pastoral presence is expected? This is where we, like Moses, need to humble ourselves, refuse to give in to the idea that we are indispensable, and structure ways to share the load. If we are in a multi-staff church, we can have different pastors and qualified lay leaders in a rotation that enables most everyone to be unplugged on sabbath days. In some churches, the pastoral staff staggers their sabbath days so there is always coverage—although that has its own downside. If the staff team is not able to practice together that means that while one staff person is out, others are working and filling up their inboxes, which is just not the same as everyone unplugging from work and resting at the same time. You will need to decide together if the upside of this approach outweighs the downsides.

If you are a solo pastor, the role of being present for pastoral emergencies can be shared with elders, deacons, or trained Stephen ministers. In order to practice sabbath we are all going to have to find ways to make ourselves dispensable—in the best sense of the word—and we are going to have to intentionally identify and prepare others to be present for what's needed in the body of Christ. This can actually turn into a wonderful opportunity to practice the priesthood of all believers.

Of course, this also means we will have to train congregants not to see us as indispensable and, God forbid, not to see our presence at their bedside as more prestigious or important than another pastor's or lay leader's presence. We will have to challenge any sort of celebrity mindset that fosters a belief that they are more special or get better care just because the senior pastor is the one who comes to visit, rather than the associate pastor or the lay elder or deacon. There are all kinds of intentionality that need to be brought to sabbath-keeping in community to enable leaders as well as congregants to enjoy the necessary benefits of this crucial practice. And we simply must accept the fact that a leader's choices really do set the tone for everyone in significant ways.

In the community I lead, we are very committed to our practice of sabbath. We teach it. We model it. We practice it. We live it. It has been that way from the beginning. But early on, when my own practice of sabbath was fledgling at best, I was still experimenting a bit. It didn't take long for me to figure out that anything I did or didn't do that could be considered inconsistent with our stated commitment to sabbath (or any value we hold for that matter) was inordinately impactful. We all knew Sunday was our sabbath and that no one was expected to work on the sabbath. We also knew that the sixth day (for us this was Saturday) was also important for accomplishing the work of being human. But still, early on, there were times when some of us did do some work on the sabbath, sneaking in an email or a text here and there.

Looking back, I know I contributed to real confusion by deciding at times that something was urgent enough that it needed to be dealt with right then, or I was self-centered enough to just want to get something off my head, no matter how receiving an email from me on the sabbath might affect anyone else! But here's the thing I had to learn and accept: *any* decision I made to open the door to working on the sabbath caused others to feel they needed to spring into action. This is the nature of leadership—speed of the leader, speed of the team.

Eventually I learned my lesson and just stopped doing any emailing or texting with staff on Sundays. No matter what, I just don't do it. Even though we teach about sabbath and the commitment is stated in our employee handbook, that is not what makes it real. What makes it real is what we actually do— particularly what I do, as the senior leader in our ministry. *That* is how everyone knows it's really okay to unplug from work and technology on the sabbath. This is the privilege and responsibility of leadership.

What Your Soul Wants to Say to God

So, what do you think? Are you up for the challenge of unplugging from technology on the sabbath and experiencing a new level of freedom?

If you have not done so already, begin by experimenting with how you handle technology, observing the difference it makes. Notice the difference between

- *going for a walk with your phone or without your phone.*
- *having your phone with you over lunch with a friend or leaving it in the car.*
- *having your phone with you on a date night or leaving it at home altogether.*
- *getting dressed with the TV on or off, driving while listening to the news or a podcast, or not.*
- *sleeping with your phone by your bed or keeping it in another room.*
- *having solitude with your phone nearby, in the off mode, or in another room.*
- *having your phone nearby while writing sermons, prepping for a meeting, or reading, OR leaving it out of sight and sound until you are at a good stopping point.*

What do you notice about your energy, your attention span, your presence to God and to others? Be honest. Speak to God about this.

How do you respond to the idea of tech shabbat? Don't rush into anything; just notice how it feels to consider this as a possibility and if you feel any need or desire for this.

6

SABBATH *as* DELIGHT

• ● ◦

If you refrain from trampling the sabbath . . .
if you call the sabbath a delight and the holy day
of the LORD *honorable . . . then you shall take delight in*
the LORD, *and I will make you ride upon the heights.*

ISAIAH 58:13-14

I LOVE TO PUTZ, to putter around. It's taken me a long time to admit this—probably because I think of it as something elderly men do in their garages—but now that I have encountered others for whom "putzing" is also a delight, I am more willing to just come right out and say it. Over the years I have wondered why I get so much pleasure and satisfaction from this and I think it is because, like you, I live my days moving from one thing to the next in a highly scheduled fashion, without a lot of freedom to just let things unfold. I also think putzing represents a universal longing for home. I am gone from home a lot—for work and other reasons—and the joy of putzing is really the joy of being in my home *with time* to simply attend to my human self and life by doing things I enjoy in whatever order I want to do them.

For me, putzing might mean reading for pleasure for as long as I want to (delicious!) and then dozing when I get sleepy; writing a handwritten note to someone who is on my heart, just because; trying out a new recipe because it sounds good and I have the time; dropping everything and going for a walk at just the right moment when the air is soft, and the sun is at just the right spot in the sky. It might be bringing order to my desk by sifting through and slowly reading what has piled up there, and being thoughtful with it; enjoying a spur-of-the-moment gathering with friends or family, using only what we already have in our kitchens so no one has to go to a store; picking up my journal and taking time to reflect on the events of the week—where God was with me, where God felt absent, paying attention to emotions or questions that stirred in response and letting God into that. Or maybe savoring a slow, thoughtful conversation with my spouse that would have gone much differently if we had tried it during the week when we were both exhausted and stressed.

For someone else, these sorts of delights might include going for a long run, playing a pickup game of basketball with whoever is around, going fishing, working with their hands and getting lost in a creative process, writing poetry, or playing a musical instrument. For this Myers-Briggs *P* (Perceiving), part of the joy of all this is the fact that the day can just unfold according to simple wants and desires rather than everything having to be planned out. For Myers-Briggs *J*s (Judging), it might be more delightful to have a schedule and a plan. But the relevant question is, What is it that delights you? Do you even know? Can you believe God wants to give it to you and then receive it? As Rabbi Heschel points out, "The Sabbath is not dedicated solely to spiritual goals. It is a day of the soul as well as the body; comfort and pleasure are an integral part of the Sabbath observance. Man in his entirety, all his faculties, must share its blessing."

FREE TO BE NEIGHBORLY

Commentators have noted that the fourth commandment about keeping the sabbath is a bridge—we could call it a hinge point—between the first three commandments, which refer to our relationship with God, and the next six commandments, which refer to our life with others, particularly family, friends and neighbors. Sabbath brings us home to our lives as they have been given to us by God, inviting us to inhabit more fully and freely our real lives in a particular geographical location with particular people.

Most days of the week we are on such tight timelines that we find ourselves roaring in and out of driveways, making haste through apartment hallways and parking lots as we try to get groceries in on the way home from work, rushing to accomplish the tasks associated with being human, and trying to facilitate an optimal life for our children by running them here, there, and everywhere. But, on the sabbath . . . ah, the sabbath. Because we don't have any place else to be and because we have consciously set aside work, productivity, and all that typically drives our frantic schedules, we have the opportunity to move slower, take time to greet our neighbors, stand around and talk for a while, or even pull out lawn chairs and sit together for a spell.

In this sabbath state of mind, as we are being resuscitated by God's gift of rest, we may have enough capacity to take an interest in others and enjoy them rather than being so focused on hoarding our time and energy. In this sabbath state of being, we may have enough capacity to stop and be present to our neighbors (however we might define *neighbor* on any given day), rather than rushing into our dwellings, barely able to muster a wave. In fact, when Jesus asserts his lordship over the sabbath (Mark 2:25-28) he places a higher value on being kind and neighborly—even helping your neighbor get his cow out of the ditch, if needed—than keeping any legalistic prohibitions. So when this impulse to be neighborly strikes on the sabbath, stop and do what it tells you.

Recently I have been spending time with our neighbor across the street whose dear husband passed away after a short and startling bout with cancer. Most times these little visits are very simple—making extra of whatever we are eating and taking over a little care package, sharing a sweet treat, or putting a mum on her porch and checking in. Most often these little stop-bys happen on Sundays when I am more relaxed, don't have much of a schedule to keep, and my energies are being replenished. Often she invites me in and we sit together as she shares about whatever moment she is in in her grieving process or the practicalities of trying to figure out how to live without him. These moments always feel like sabbath moments to me. Time slows down as I am simply present with another human being who is in a slightly different place on the human journey than I am. There is really nothing I can do for her except be, and I know it makes a difference. It is the fullness of time—sabbath time. This is the good stuff and I just don't want to miss it!

FROM EXHAUSTION TO GRATITUDE

Oftentimes I arrive at the sabbath so tired that it's hard to really enjoy anything. This is discouraging at times but I find that if I can give in to my tiredness without guilt and let it be what it is—allowing the rest to come—gratitude seeps up from the ground of my being in the most natural way, like water seeping up from a well-watered earth. As this God-given rest soaks my soul, there are these tender sprouts of gratitude poking their way up through the surface of my consciousness, and I find myself feeling grateful for aspects of my life I have taken for granted all week when life was too full and yet empty all at the same time. Gratitude for the simple things (like how good my coffee tastes in the morning), as well as time to savor the bigger things (home, family, God's dear presence in my life), allow my heart to swell with joy.

Eventually, gratitude turns into delight as I engage life's simple pleasures from a more rested place—especially those gifts and pleasures that can't be bought and marketed in a consumeristic culture. And from there, worship is rather inevitable. But here's the thing: often what takes place in our churches simply doesn't meet what sabbath time is really all about, which is another way in which church life can actually work against a sabbath life. Tilden Edwards makes this challenging and convicting statement:

> Corporate worship can be the pinnacle of Christian sabbath, but it is not the sabbath. It is unrealistic to expect people to be fully present in liturgy when it is surrounded by rushed, distracting activities of every kind. A dulled or distracted mind cannot worship with any depth. Preachers

and worship leaders sense this, but rather than focusing on people's sabbath time surrounding the service, they instead sometimes might try ever more desperately to force people's attention during the service through dramatic or frivolously humorous sermons, and through exciting music or other elements that can easily cross the line from worship to consumer entertainment. Such efforts are bound to fail spiritually in the end . . . because they cannot do for people what people must do for themselves.

Embracing a sabbath life together may challenge some of our most basic assumptions about what Sundays are even all about.

When sabbath was first given, the emphasis was on rest. Then when Moses reiterated the Ten Commandments in Deuteronomy, there was an additional emphasis on remembering—remembering God's goodness, God's faithfulness, and God's liberating power. "Remember that you were a slave in the land of Egypt, and the LORD your God brought you out from there with a mighty hand and an outstretched arm; therefore the LORD your God commanded you to keep the sabbath day" (Deuteronomy 5:15). Sabbath itself became an act of worship—for the Israelites and for us—renewing our faith in God's power and intention to deliver us in whatever way is needed today.

Today, Christians have moved communal worship to Sundays in celebration of Jesus' resurrection victory over death, and this theme of remembrance is carried over because it is fulfilled in Christ. The Israelites remembering how God delivered them from their bondage has now morphed into us as New Testament Christians remembering how Christ accomplished victory for us over sin and death. Dorothy Bass writes,

68

This vortex of dying and rising—Jesus' and ours in him—is the *paschal mystery.* Christians still tell it and taste it, especially when we gather for worship on Sunday. Christ's *Pascha*—the word for the Jewish passage from bondage to freedom that Christians apply to Christ's passing from death to life—was the center of the weekly worship for the earliest Christians.

Hopefully we have a community of faith with whom to share this fulsome experience of worship—ceasing our work, which enables us to rest, which creates space for remembrance and delighting in God's good gifts. And it all adds up to joyful worship in which we experience once again communion with the risen Christ and our brothers and sisters in his body, the church—an essential part of the Christian sabbath.

What this may mean is that in a sabbath community, we strive for worship to be carried out simply and restfully rather than making it a lot of work for anyone. We may decide to do away with the big productions that require early morning call times for the worship team and instead let it be enough to remember with gratitude, to attribute to God all the praise God deserves, and then to send everyone home to *continue their worship* by resting in God and delighting in God's best gifts.

MENDING OUR TATTERED LIVES

Something else I have noticed throughout my years of sabbath-keeping is that it is not just feelings of joy and delight that are heightened on this set-apart day. Oddly enough, we may be surprised by feelings of loss and emptiness that become more pronounced and difficult to tolerate on this day. Hard things we thought we had put to rest may ambush our awareness, along with the pain associated with them. Unresolved issues and relationships may come up from the deep, assailing us with feelings of disappointment, disillusionment, and a sense of powerlessness to do anything about it. If we are empty nesters or unmarried, if a marriage has ended or a spouse has died, perhaps feelings of loneliness feel unbearable, and the day stretches out interminably as we think about couples and families spending the day together in loving and intimate ways.

Over and over again I have experienced the bubbling up of harder emotions on the sabbath, and at first it felt like a betrayal. *I mean, really, isn't the sabbath supposed to be a time of unmitigated rest and delight?* I have wondered. *What's going on here? Am I doing something wrong?*

There is good reason for why this happens, and it is helpful to be prepared. On the sabbath we are without the normal distractions of busyness, work, and productivity; we are more present to our lives as they really are, which means we are more present to the gifts as well as the pain and the emptiness. Most of us have at least a couple of painful realities in our lives that will probably not be fixed or resolved this side of heaven; I know I do. During the week I am often able to keep them somewhat outside of my awareness simply because I am busier, but on the sabbath there is no buffer—these harder realities are right there.

What is most helpful here is to realize that emotions that seem to be in opposition to one another are often actually two sides of the same coin. Taking time to remember the good things creates space for memories of hard things as well. Delighting in God's good gifts might also put us in touch with gifts

70

we have not been given and had always hoped for. A sense of fullness in one area might also put us in touch with emptiness in another area.

Part of the human condition is that we either feel a full range of human emotion or we cut ourselves off from our emotions so we don't feel much at all. Unfortunately, we don't get to have it both ways—feeling only the emotions we want to feel (love, joy, pleasure, passion, bliss, satisfaction) while cutting ourselves off from the emotions we don't want to feel (anger, frustration, resentment, sadness, grief, longing). On the sabbath we are stripped of the ways in which work, productivity, consumerism, and dopamine hits from being on social media function to keep our awareness of more painful realities at bay. When we withdraw from all of that on the sabbath, other levels of awareness may bubble to the surface and we are present with the hard things as well. That is not always easy, but sabbath does create space for God to be with us, to comfort and help us make meaning of those things that seem so difficult and mean*ingless*. This offers a very deep kind of replenishment and re-membering—that is, giving God the opportunity to "mend our tattered lives" and put us back together again in the way that only God can.

ACCEPTANCE, NOT DENIAL

On the sabbath we may be tempted to run back to our usual distractions, and if we are not paying attention we might give in. All of us will give in from time to time, but don't waste energy feeling guilty; determine to learn from the experience and do something more productive next time. If we *can* catch ourselves before giving in to distraction and numbing behaviors, we can make the choice to *be with God with what is* and experience another kind of rest—the rest that comes through acceptance rather than denial. There is no better day than sabbath to let God lead us into a place of acceptance and to practice trusting God with the great unfixables of our lives. We can remember how God has been with us in past difficulties and choose to have faith that God will meet us again.

Here are some elements of resting in God with hard things on the sabbath:

- First of all, acknowledge the hard thing and face it for what it really is—in all of its ramifications. Speak to God directly about it in prayer or in a journal. This step alone is very different from denial and numbing.

- Feel all the feels. Rather than holding back or holding anything in (which we often have to do for various reasons) allow the safety of sabbath time to create space for your tears, and cry them if God gives them. Express anger, or any other emotions that come, in some appropriate way.

- If available, talk to a spiritual friend or a spouse who can simply be present to what you are experiencing, being with you and bearing witness to the pain without trying to fix or problem solve.

- Let the emotions take their course, trusting that you will move through and come to an end of the intensity—at least for now. Perhaps, by God's grace, you will experience something like the blue skies that appear after the storm.

- Do something life giving and comforting for your human self. Breathe deeply, go for a walk with a loved one, take a nap under a quilt or blanket, have a quiet cup of tea . . . anything that leaves you feeling held and cared for.

Many of us don't realize that we are weary (and volatile) from holding so much in. Sabbath can be just the opportunity we need to stop working so hard at holding everything in and rest with God, even with the hard stuff. It takes courage to "go there," but God promises to be with us even in our lowest moments, and we will never know how God will meet us until we try. "Blessed are those who mourn, for they will be comforted" (Matthew 5:4).

One more thing—while we are on this earth we will always be moving in and out of feelings of loneliness, incompleteness, and being cut off from the union and communion we seek. That is a part of being human, and our awareness of this reality of the human condition may be more pronounced on the sabbath, again simply due to the lack of so many distractions. There is an exquisite little poem from Hafiz that begins with the words "Don't surrender your loneliness so quickly / Let it cut more deep." These lines are arresting precisely because they are so counterintuitive in a world where we would do almost anything to run from our loneliness. And yet the final lines of the poem offer us a way of actually embracing our loneliness in a spiritually productive way rather than running from it: "Something missing in my heart tonight / Has made my eyes so soft / My voice so tender / My need of God absolutely clear."

What delights you? Really, what delights you? Take a moment to get specific about this and allow yourself to dream of a day that had more of this in it.

Have you ever rested long enough to move from exhaustion to gratitude to worship? Remember what that was like and see if you can envision letting that happen once a week.

Is there anything in your life right now that feels so hard you might be avoiding it by giving in to distraction, emotional numbing, or denial? How might sabbath offer an opportunity to enter more fully into the rest that comes from trust and acceptance? Are you open to this?

How can sabbath guide you in being with loneliness in a way that draws you into intimacy with God?

7

SABBATH *and the* SEASONS *of* LIFE

● ● ●

Our Sabbath project grew out of a desire to see what would
happen if, on one day out of seven, we stopped working, striving,
and hurrying. The result of this experience was clarifying,
expansive, freeing. It was also annoying, difficult and odd. Our
house was a perpetual wreck. We fell behind on work and
domestic tasks. Our day-long togetherness sometimes drove
us crazy. Yet we wouldn't trade the experience for anything.

MARYANN McKIBBEN DANA

INVARIABLY WHEN I SPEAK about the sabbath, someone will
raise a hand and ask about the challenges of practicing sabbath
in a family with young children or they might even make a
statement like, "I take my sabbath on Mondays while my kids are
at school." If they ask what I think about that, my first response
is to say that I completely understand—family life is sometimes

part of what we feel weary *from* and we may be afraid that the effort required to harness a whole family to practice sabbath would take more from us than it could possibly replenish.

At the same time, I always feel slightly uncomfortable upon hearing this for the simple reason that sabbath is and always has been a practice for people to enter into with those closest to them. So while I understand why people might gravitate toward practicing sabbath while children are at school, I cannot recommend it. Instead I believe we are called to explore sharing sabbath with our families and others with whom we share our lives. Being open, curious, and experimental about how we might do this is simply another aspect of the communal nature of sabbath that warrants our attention and intention.

Of course, there are other seasons when sabbath-keeping may feel challenging for different reasons—such as seasons when we are loving and caring for aging parents and sabbath seems impossible in a completely different way. And sometimes, because of an undue emphasis on family in our churches, people who are in seasons of singleness and/or living alone can sometimes feel left out. But sabbath is a gift of God for the people of God *in all seasons of our lives* and in whatever stage of the human journey we find ourselves. Remember: solitude, silence, and retreat are the practices that create space for private time with God; sabbath is a different opportunity altogether.

SABBATH IN THE COLLEGE AND YOUNG ADULT YEARS

Sabbath is a gift for all ages and stages, but it will be experienced differently throughout the various seasons of our lives.

It is good to be open to this rather than getting stuck in assuming sabbath will look the same in every season. Jessica is a gifted young nurse practitioner and caring midwife who serves long hours in underresourced communities. She describes her own sabbath progression through college and beyond.

When I first began practicing Sabbath, I was a sophomore in college. Sabbath practice appealed to me for three reasons. Firstly, I was increasingly aware of the toll the combination of my perfectionism and a hypercompetitive academic environment were taking on me, and I welcomed the physical and spiritual rest that Sabbath offered. Secondly, setting aside time for Sabbath rest was countercultural, a witness to my overscheduled and stressed peers: Christianity offers rest, not just rules! And thirdly, "Sabbathing," as my friends and I called it, was a mark of Christian maturity, a sign of having transcended daily stressors and reached deeper trust in God. Subconsciously, taking a day off to celebrate Sabbath was something to be good at, and I have always liked being good at things.

I would spend hours in prayer, wander through the parts of campus I normally rushed past on my way to class, have leisurely brunches with friends, and hide my laptop and books so I would not be tempted to work. I would also routinely stay up until two, three, or four o'clock in the morning on Saturday nights, frantically rushing to finish problems sets and essays, before collapsing into bed, exhausted but proud of my effort. As much of a gift as Sabbath was in those early days—marked with succulent afternoon naps, intimate moments with friends, and precious times of prayer—I still saw it as something to earn by working hard enough all week.

Since then, I have received the Sabbath as a gift more or less openhandedly, depending on my season of life. The more I understand the Sabbath as a gift, the more I prepare myself to receive the Sabbath instead of merely clearing my schedule for twenty-four hours and hoping for the best. (Though even in the weeks I can hardly manage that, God still meets me.) I now choose a time to stop working the night before, light a candle, and physically clean my space before going to bed. I also change my sheets—both because I love the fresh detergent smell and as a sign to put away the old week and enter into rest. During my Sabbath, I typically completely shut off my laptop and phone unless I have planned a time for a call with a loved one. As a single person and an introvert working in a deeply relational and emotionally intimate field, I am acutely aware of my need to steward both times of solitude and times of community.

My Sabbath is often bookended by community (church in the morning, and an extended call or dinner with a loved one in the evening), giving me space during the day for a solitary long run, slow reading, cooking something more complex than the weekdays allow, or just sitting quietly on the porch. I know some single people struggle with loneliness on the Sabbath, but I have actually discovered it to be a time of fullness—through the experience of intimacy with God as I rest in God, and also by being very intentional about planning for meaningful connection with loved ones. The more I let go of Sabbath-as-reward or Sabbath-as-self-care and embrace Sabbath-as-gift, the more I experience God sustaining and transforming me in it.

SABBATH WITH CHILDREN AND TEENS

One of my regrets about my own practice of sabbath is that we started it somewhat late in our family's life, when our kids were teenagers. By the time we became convinced of its importance and decided we were going to go for it, our kids were well established in some of their own patterns and priorities. Honestly, it didn't feel right to impose this new discipline on them midstream just because we were feeling called to it; we did not want the sabbath to become an obligation rather than a gift, a battle rather than a delight, so I started practicing sabbath first and soon my husband joined me. This meant drawing some new boundaries as we tried not to work, shop, attend sporting events, do budgeting, scheduling, wedding planning, or have hard disciplinary conversations on the sabbath.

One of the most difficult decisions we made had to do with traveling sports teams that played on Sundays, which was our sabbath. At the time one of our daughters played on a traveling soccer team that held their games on Sundays. So we made the tough choice that we would not be packing chairs, coolers, and water bottles to spend half the day on the sidelines of youth soccer games, because that felt too much like business as usual versus the restful day sabbath was supposed to be. We lovingly explained our call to sabbath as we were understanding it and let her know she was free to make her own choice about whether to play sports on Sundays if she could work out getting rides to and from. She did choose to play, and the rides did indeed seem to work themselves out. This was an adjustment, to be sure, but because we supported her athletics in so many other ways, we felt fine about it—and in the end it was not really that big a deal.

Ironically, when this same daughter went to a Christian college that adhered to the principle of not playing sports on Sundays, she experienced for herself the benefits of having one day a week when she was not defined by what she could do as a competitive athlete. As an All-American soccer player who was captain of several national championship teams, she acknowledged that she benefited from resting the competitive, hard-working part of herself and allowing other aspects of herself to emerge and flourish. How much better that she figured this out for herself through her own experience rather than us imposing it on her and risking forming within her a resentment of the sabbath.

Of course, when we began our sabbath practice in a family full of busy teenagers there were some tense and disgruntled moments, but once our daughters began to get used to it they seemed to really enjoy the differences that were present on that day. They warmed to the fact that I was around all day and that we could talk, take walks, go on bike rides, and cook our favorite foods. They loved the fact that we could all take naps and go with the flow. They, too, began to sense and eventually articulate their need for a day to rest and experienced their own disappointment when something in their lives or ours robbed us of this important time. And it was the nicest surprise when even as teenagers, they let their bosses at their minimum wage jobs know that they could not work on Sundays.

These days it is a great joy to see them, along with their husbands, learn to love the sabbath and wrestle with it in their young families. When I get tearful about the fact that our late-in-the-game attempts at sabbath-keeping might have fallen short and robbed them of something important, they assure me that what we modeled by practicing sabbath ourselves and welcoming them to participate in whatever way they chose, instilled in them a desire to figure it out for themselves when the time was right. In fact, our oldest daughter, Charity, agreed to write about her experience in our family and now with her young family as she and her husband, Kyle, have sought to order their lives around this life-giving practice:

It wasn't until my early thirties that I began to feel the need for a sabbath practice for myself. Up until that point, my life had been spilling over with school and work, friends and family, activities and social commitments. As my weeks filled up with more work and responsibility, I compensated by packing my weekends to the brim with play and travel. My youthful response to a slew of new adult responsibilities meant that I was a bit out of control, running nonstop without any noticeable consequences. The truth is that at the time I loved it. I look back on those days with much fondness for the work I got to be a part of and all that I learned in my first job, the long days spent on boats and weekends living out of a duffle bag, the energy that allowed me to organize and host countless gatherings, and the friendships that were forged by showing up anytime and anywhere.

It wasn't until I had lived without limits long enough to reach a place where sabbath was something I needed and desperately wanted, that I was willing to actually consider it. My longing for more of God sent me seeking to integrate spiritual practices that would sustain me as a young mother but also help me cultivate the quality of presence I experienced in my older spiritual friends and mentors. With two small children and one on the way, my ideas about sabbath were quite disconnected from what was actually possible. Fully aware of my children's endless needs and energy, the thought of having a set-apart day for rest and enjoyment felt similar to the dream of the perfect family vacation: you desperately need the time away and think you have this great idea for a destination, you want to believe it's possible to go away and come back feeling restored—yet, inevitably, you come back not only tired but also ashamed to admit that you might even be disappointed.

I didn't want to set myself up for that kind of disappointment, but I also couldn't shake the longing I had for a way of life that works. Sabbath couldn't just be for seasons when life is manageable; sabbath seemed to be a gift for those whose life was unmanageable! I had spent years cultivating the good gifts in my life, but these good gifts were starting to wear me out. There were not enough hours in the day, days in the week, or weekends in the year to fit everything I was trying to squeeze into it. Our calendar was full of all the best things and yet we were still not meeting relational expectations, we were traveling most weekends, and having trouble being really present in our neighborhood. Too often we were up late with friends and up early with babies, unwilling to really look at the toll it was taking. We didn't want to miss anything, so we just kept packing it all in—unaware that what we were actually missing were the gifts that come from living within our human limitations.

From this depleted place I started to let myself envision a weekly rhythm that would allow me to receive the gifts of my life instead of racing to keep up with them. I needed permission to regularly care for myself and experience those moments as God's care for me. I knew I would struggle to step away from all there was to do and let go of all the unmet expectations, yet it was hard for me to believe that at the end of a week it was enough—that I was enough. I longed for God to meet me in these places—the places where gratitude takes root, where a beautiful quality of presence can be cultivated, where we experience a deep trust in God's love and goodness to us.

So, rather than giving up on vacations and sabbaths, I decided to reframe them. Starting with how we talk about them, my husband, Kyle, and I began to articulate a vision for what was most needed and most doable. Much like shifting our thinking and ex-pectations from having a family vacation to taking a family trip, a similar shift was necessary as we embarked on our sabbath practice. Instead of seeing it as a day of rest, we looked for ways to create a day for being. It's a subtle shift, but in this season when my intention is to be present—to my family, to myself, to God—this shift helps us create a sabbath practice that is attainable. I asked questions like:

How can I be more present to myself, to my family, to God?

What is the work we most need a break from?

What are the individual needs for each family member that can be attended to in our sabbath practices?

How can our family enjoy our home, our yard, and each other?

What are some of the easiest ways our family can spend time together?

How would it feel to have a day where we take a break from our usual activities and enter into a different way of being together—one that practices a slower pace for the purpose of settling into a more grounded experience of ourselves and a more joyful con-nection to each other and our Creator?

How would we communicate and set expectations for those outside of our family's rhythm?

The answers to these questions are not ones I can find on my own; they can only be found as I trust God's goodness and believe he will meet me in the space I am carving out. I have also found that if I am holding too tightly to my own desires and preconceived ideas, I can't receive what God wants to give me. When I focus less on getting rest in the ways I might typically expect, God can bring about replenishment in ways I wouldn't expect. Instead of stressing about exactly how I will get the solitude I need, I can let the day unfold and watch for the gift of twenty to thirty minutes where I can slip away or just sit quietly. Often there are sabbaths where the nap I longed for didn't come but that sent me to bed earlier, which set me up even better for the next day. Or perhaps I was interrupted reading the book I chose, but the book my children want me to read speaks to my heart in a different way. Sometimes the break I think I need from my kids might simply be a break from our more stressful ways of interacting. It's amazing the kind of relational shifts that can happen when outside commitments and expectations are lifted. There are countless expectations that tired parents can bring into sabbath, but a fruitful prayer that we pray often in the Transforming Center can also be applied to this set-apart day: "God, we ask not for what we want, but for what you know we need."

There can be tension between what a parent most needs and what a child most needs, but the balance is worth finding. It is good for our children to see us more and more fully as human beings, starting at a young age. In all of our rhythms and practices, we are teaching our children how to open themselves more fully to God and the best way to show them is to live it. Our freedom in Christ will be our children's freedom in Christ. If we cannot break free from our own striving and achieving and performing, how much harder will it be for our children? By prioritizing self-care in concrete ways—resting or playing or creating—I honor the person God created me to be, and in doing so, I give my children permission to honor the people God has made them to be.

One of the greatest joys we have experienced is helping our three little ones discover the gift of this day for themselves. Regardless of how our week has gone, sabbath is a weekly opportunity to see each of my children with fresh eyes. Our interactions are not about what we have to do or where we have to go but rather what we'd like to do and where we'd like to go. I notice and appreciate what they choose to do when they are alone. I am more present to their rambling stories which reveal what they care about and how they are experiencing the world. What a gift it is to see your children as they are and to encourage them to rest in that identity each and every week.

When our oldest son, Finn, was nine years old, we started talking to him about his personal sabbath practice and how to start experimenting with the day for himself. As the pressure with school and friends and activities builds each year, we have come to see how much this little soul needs a day of rest. Maybe he wants to curl up with a book or go outside to take photos. Maybe we go on a family bike ride or maybe he'd like to be alone. He takes joy in healthy homemade food so sometimes I ask him to help me think toward our meals for that week. We loosen the reins on things like household chores, only asking that we help each other enough that the work doesn't fall to just one or two people. For a while we have been doing church on Saturday nights, so on Sunday morning he never makes his bed, sometimes stays in his pajamas most of the day and rarely brushes his hair! We are now going to church on Sunday mornings, but we don't fuss about what he wears or how he looks; that is just not a priority for us on sabbath. Finn's personality (like many of the rest of us!) needs a day where nothing is being asked of him and no one is asking him to be anything beyond where he is right now. On sabbath days we try to encourage anything that helps our son discover and settle into himself and into our home, so he can breathe deep the love of God through our family, letting go of any "oughts" and "shoulds" to see what might bring him joy on that day.

As parents, we also have tried to let go of the "oughts" and "shoulds." Not everyone in our life practices sabbath so it took some time to casually work that language into those relationships. I started by just slipping it into little chats about our weekend: "The kids had games on Saturday, we got some yard work done and then we really took the sabbath to rest." Or in talking about a busy week: "Yeah, this week has a lot for us, but I am grateful because we have protected the sabbath so our family will get what we need then."

It was really helpful to us to have close friends and family who knew that we were working to orient our week toward a sabbath practice. This meant that the ways we chose to get together on the weekends (even on sabbath) didn't conflict with our intentions to be more fully present to God and each other on that day.

We also stopped feeling obligated to always answer our phones or respond right away to messages or texts. If it could wait, we would reach out on Monday, often without apology or explanation. If people seemed irritated or confused about the delay, we would just tell them that we give ourselves one day a week to be more intentional about our time together. You can actually shape people's expectations of you over time in this way.

I realize now that my posture toward this practice is the biggest influence on how I perceive its outcome. If I approach sabbath honestly with God about my needs and desires, but also stay in touch with what I most long for in our family and for our children, I can hold it all before God and learn to trust his provision for each of us. In my tiredness I am tempted to grasp only what I need for myself, but out of faith I will stay open to receive what God wants to give all of us. Sabbath with growing children in the home is going to look different and feel different at each age and stage, but

I am finding that even in the unfolding there are unexpected gifts— moments I didn't even know I needed, places of gentle noticing— where God quietly reveals places he and I will revisit later. Sabbath is a very practical place for me to trust that whatever God and I can do on this day, no matter how much or how little, it is enough.

Sabbath can be hit or miss depending on many factors. We have had sweet seasons of sabbath where it comes easy, and bitter seasons where the space we are seeking to hold is met with resistance. We've had days that started with difficulty and ended with blessing, and we've had days that were so difficult they never felt redeemed. But we have also had the days where all five of us have settled into the kind of rest that both adults and children need— where we are each reminded of the gifts we have in each other, where we feel deeply loved and seen for who we are rather than what we do, and we experience the joy of accepting an invitation to a sacred rhythm given to us by the One who knows what we most need.

This brings me back around to the gift my mother gave me. As she began to practice sabbath, my sisters and I couldn't help but experience a shift. On Sundays my mom was just home. She wasn't working or writing. She wasn't in a car or on her phone. She pulled out her recipe box and made food there wasn't always time to make on other days. She would curl up on her couch with a book, but was always delighted to be interrupted by one of us looking to talk. We didn't change all of our plans and we certainly didn't value the practice for ourselves at that moment, but we were drawn to be with her on those days and a sabbath seed was planted. What this taught me is that if we truly believe sabbath is a gift from God, then let's not unwrap the gift for our children and demand they appreciate it. Let us open the gift for ourselves and live in gratitude for God's generosity toward us. Let our sabbath selves be the kind of presence that draws our children to us through our slowness, our attentiveness, our joy, our rest. May we allow our children to grow in their curiosity about the sabbath gifts that God has waiting for them. Even if it takes years for them to open it (as it did for me), each of us deserves to encounter God's goodness toward us when we are ready to receive it.

The bottom line here is that when people practice sabbath in such a way that their family is not able to engage it with them, they are missing one of the basic intentions of the practice—and that is families and communities resting together and being shaped together by the freedom, the faith, and the goodness of what God has for us. If we allow sabbath to become a discipline in which we withdraw from our families rather than choosing to do it together, children will not have the opportunity to experience sabbath time with the guidance of their parents. They will not gain the benefits of unplugging and learning how to rest and delight in God's simpler gifts that they so desperately need. The special gifts shared during sabbath time—a different quality of presence, the love that is shared in the being state rather than the doing state, the gratitude, the opportunity to rest and play and unplug and do all those things that run counter to life in our culture—will be lost to the next generation. And that is a loss too great to bear.

SEASONS OF CAREGIVING

The same is true for seasons when we are caring for aging parents, a spouse who is ill, or adult children who may have particular challenges that keep us in a caregiving role longer than we expected. The five-year season when I had the privilege of living near my parents and caring for them through their illnesses and deaths was probably the most intense season of my life, and the exhaustion was so deep I wondered if I would make it. How grateful I was that I had been practicing sabbath, though, because it helped me to know how important it was for me to carve out sabbath time, and that I still needed rest even when I couldn't always practice sabbath to the extent that I desired. One adjustment I made during this time is that I rarely turned my phone off while my parents were relying on me for their care. If I did turn off my phone in order to get some rest, I would let them know ahead of time that I was doing it and arrange for them to call my husband if they needed anything. My husband was very generous with me and very kind to them during this season, which gave me some time for necessary unplugging.

There are some really fine lines to find in this season, between the self-care caregivers really *must* attend to in order to make it for the long haul, and the invitation to share sabbath time and our sabbath self with parents who are so vulnerable during their season of diminishment. Every week I found myself needing to discern with God what that week called for. Is this going be a week when I completely crash on the sabbath and don't see my parents at all? Could I see them on Saturday so that on Sunday I would feel more free? Is this a sabbath where, after resting for part of the day, I might find myself replenished enough to give them the gift of presence? Or is this a day when I am called to push through and do what is needed even though I don't think I have anything left? All I could do was discern it week by week. There were times when I asked others to be my proxy, because knowing my parents were receiving loving attention from other family members freed me up to get the rest

I needed. And then there were times when I was able to take my sabbath way of being into time spent with them, and those were the most precious moments of all.

I am so grateful I had been avidly practicing sabbath previous to this season because I knew what the quality of sabbath time was, and at times it was a gift I could bring to them. That said, my parents never lived with us, and families who make the choice to have their parents stay in their home will have to make different choices. They may need to call on family members and other caregivers to help them get a few sabbath hours, even if not a whole twenty-four hours. Knowing about the sabbath gives us freedom and permission to be intentional about getting our own rest while also inviting us to look for ways to share sabbath time with our dear loved ones, who need to see our faces shining love on them within the sanctuary in time sabbath creates.

SEASONS OF SINGLENESS

Sometimes, in our hyper focus on families in our culture and in the church, we fail to acknowledge seasons of singleness and therefore miss the unique opportunities embedded in this season. I asked my beautiful friend Rev. Dr. Phaedra Blocker, a mature single woman who is an educator and an activist, to comment on her practice and perspective; her gentle encouragement actually applies to all of us, or at least it probably will at one time or another.

I believe one of the blessings of sabbath practice is that it serves to affirm (or perhaps reaffirm) the single person as a complete human being—without need for definition by virtue of some familial or marital relationship. The God who institutes sabbath as an essential (and statutory) practice for all creation does not create different categories or standards of sabbath for single people versus married couples. Sabbath is created for the individual first, and then the unfolding circles of community and creation. For single people, then, there is a need to cherish our own sense of being—as full, beautiful images of the Divine. We should not, as has sometimes been suggested in our cultural and faith communities, see ourselves as somehow incomplete because we do not have a marital partner and so feel that we are somehow excluded from the call and blessing of sabbath. The imago Dei that we embody is a single, complete image that was created to exist in community. And the composition of that community can rightly take many forms, all of which can be God-honoring and life-giving.

Therefore, we need to embrace the reality that sabbath was created for us, too! And we have "permission" to seek out the forms of rest and renewal that are most helpful to us, without feeling that we must participate in relational situations that are not restful or that we are somehow lacking or "less than" because we spend the time alone. And it should be emphasized that there is a great difference between being alone and being lonely. Loneliness is a symptom that we have not been able, for whatever reason, to create the ongoing relational connections that humans need in order to flourish. Being able to be alone, however, is a sign that we are grounded enough in our beings (and our Being) that we can release ourselves from connection with others for a time without fear or sense of loss—that is one of the reasons that the spiritual practice of solitude is so essential.

For those inclined to a communal sabbath experience, a long, unhurried meal with a friend (or two or more!) that allows for real conversation and connection may be just the restorative that is

91

needed. Or perhaps even a leisurely cup of coffee or tea at a local establishment that allows one to "people watch" and maybe strike up a conversation with a neighbor. I've had more than one fascinating, life-giving conversation with a random stranger that left me feeling encouraged and renewed. We were able to "rest" in our moments together and simply enjoy each other's company.

For those of us who are more introverted, a sabbath practice that nourishes our need to withdraw and recharge is often in order. The sabbath provides a wonderful opportunity each week to lean into our "wiring" in healthy ways. Declining to be drawn into communal activities and creating space to simply be with oneself and one's thoughts (or maybe a good book), preparing a simple delicious meal (or having one prepared in advance) and setting the table to sit and enjoy it (rather than eating over the sink or on the run) may offer the most restful alternative. One may also want to consider other solitary activities that feed the soul: a walk in nature, engaging in art-making of some sort (even if it's just singing along with some of your favorite music or dancing like no one is watching because, well, no one is!), or relishing in an uninterrupted nap. It is a day of rest, after all!

What are the unique challenges and opportunities for sabbath embedded in the season of life you are in right now? Take some time to reflect on this.

    If you are in college or graduate school, how might sabbath be a gift to you in the midst of the intensity of academic life? How can you pace yourself and your studies in order to practice sabbath realistically? Do you have friends who might want to practice with you?

    If you are the parent of young children and have a desire to incorporate sabbath into your family's life, take time to reflect on these questions from Charity's story:

- *What constitutes "work" for you (and/or the person you parent with) that could be removed from sabbath? What is the work each of you most needs a break from? How can you take that work for each other or eliminate/minimize it for that day?*

- *What are some of the easiest ways your family spends time together? What are the activities you can all enjoy? How can you avoid unnecessary conflict? Where are the places and what are the activities that cultivate a loving way of being together?*

- *What individual needs for each family member can be attended to on this day? How will you attend to needs that seem to be in contradiction with each other?*

- *How will you communicate and set expectations for those outside your family's rhythm?*

If you are a parent of teens, how might you practice within your family in such a way that there is a winsome invitation but no coercion?

If you are caring for aging parents in this season of your life, how can sabbath be experienced as an opportunity to replenish but also to shine the light of love on them?

How do you respond to the idea that sabbath affirms the single person as a complete human being? How can you affirm this in the community you are a part of?

8

SHAPING SABBATH

● ● ●

Sabbath is not simply the pause that refreshes,
it is the pause that transforms.

WALTER BRUEGGEMANN

I AM A BETTER PERSON on the sabbath. I am not as stressed. I move slower, talk slower, and listen better. I am kinder, more patient, more loving, and more grateful—for the big things and the small things. I am more in love with my life and the people God has given me than on any other day of the week. Somehow, in a way I cannot explain, I come back to myself and to what's most important. I sink and settle into the gifts of my life and savor them with abandon.

I am really not sure how all this happens, but on the sabbath I am more at home in my humanity, more satisfied, and less driven. I am insanely happy to putz around and just *be*, letting the day unfold. In this quieter, slower pace with fewer distractions, I am often able to plumb the deeper well at the center of my being, and from that place say true things to God—things that surprise me, things that need more time in order to come to the surface and form themselves into words, things that keep my relationship with God true, fresh, and alive.

It amazes me, really, that a person who is as driven and distractible as I am, can settle in like this, and I know the ability to do this only comes now after years of practice and pressing through the hard parts. Truly, I wish I could be the person I am on the sabbath all the time!

To what can we attribute all this betterment? While most of us have heard about sabbath and have maybe even attempted it to some extent, I'm not sure we fully understand how transformative and essential it is. It is a spiritual practice that opens us to God's transforming work, enabling us to be the kind of people we want to be on this earth. If we understood this, I think we would take it more seriously.

Like all spiritual disciplines, sabbath-keeping is a means of grace—a way of opening to the transforming work of God beyond anything we can accomplish for ourselves. I cannot will myself to be the person I experience myself to be on the sabbath, but I can open myself to it so God can come in and do what only God can do. As Rabbi Heschel puts it, "Every seventh day a miracle comes to pass, the resurrection of the soul."

FREE TO BE

So, what does sabbath-keeping actually form in us, not only as individuals but as communities of faith? What are we freed *for*? We are freed to love and be loved, to experience ourselves valued and blessed just for being. Free to delight in gifts that money can't buy and experience them as being enough. Free to rest ourselves in God and live on God's own terms for us. Most of us don't even know what to do with that much freedom and it can be quite life changing!

One of the main things we are freed *for* on the sabbath is to simply be human—to honor the body's need for rest, the spirit's need for replenishment, and the soul's need to delight itself in God for God's own sake. It begins with the willingness to acknowledge the limits of our humanness and to live more graciously within the order of things. And the first order of things is that we are creatures living in the presence of our Creator, the One who knows and loves us better than we know and love ourselves. *This is especially important for leaders* who, in a celebrity culture, are often put on pedestals and seen as superhuman. Even though other people might insist on seeing us as superhuman, we know better and simply must put a stop to it—at least on the sabbath.

By establishing a sabbath practice, we affirm and accept the fact that God is the only one who is infinite, and we are finite. This means we live within the physical limits of time and space, strength and energy. There are limits to our relational, emotional, mental, and spiritual capacities. By being faithful to a sabbath practice, we are saying in a very concrete way, "God is the only one who can be all things to all people; I am not. God is the only one who can be in two places at once; I am not. God is the one who never sleeps; I am not."

Our resistance and/or our dismissive attitude toward sabbath is often related to an unwillingness to acknowledge and live within the limits of our humanity, to honor our finiteness, to confront the nasty lie that we are indispensable. On some level we may be convinced that the world cannot go on without us, even for a day. Or we might believe there are certain tasks and activities that are more significant than the delights that God is wanting to share with us on this day. Like the Israelites, we struggle to believe that God can and will provide for us if we stop for one day doing all we think is needed to provide for ourselves. This is a grandiosity we indulge to our own peril.

Sabbath, on the other hand, marks out a path that enables us to live humbly within the limits of being human by letting go of our relentless human striving at least one day a week so we can nurture our human being-ness versus our human doing. This becomes our confession each and every time we enter in: *I am human. I am finite. I have limits. Thank you, God, for the rhythms you put in place for my good.*

Can't you just feel the freedom contained within these statements? Why not stop and practice saying them out loud right now?

A SPIRITUALITY OF LIMITS

There is something deeply spiritual about honoring the limitations of our existence as human, physical bodies in a world of time and space. There is a peace that descends on our lives when we accept what is real rather than always pushing beyond our limits. There is something about being gracious and accepting and gentle with ourselves once a week that enables us to be gracious and accepting and gentle with others too. There is a freedom that comes from being who we are in God, resting *in* God and resting *with* God, that eventually enables us to bring something truer to the world than all of our relentless striving. We touch something more real in ourselves and others than what we are all able to produce. We touch our very being in God that carries with it "limits that are part of God's original act of making us, which he called 'good.'"

Our limits are not a surprise to God, nor are they a disappointment. Our tendency to reject human limits by pretending they don't exist or pushing beyond them in ways that are detrimental to self and others is as old as the creation narrative; to accept our finiteness and live graciously within the particularity of how we have been created is to actually honor the One who made us.

This is what we witnessed in the radical choice American gymnast Simone Biles made during the 2021 Tokyo Olympics. An athlete who has routinely seemed to defy limits, Biles came to the realization that she had hit up against real limits, so she pulled out of four Olympic finals—she knew she was "off" mentally and needed to prioritize her mental health. Having come into the Tokyo games under immense pressure to win five gold medals, she had been haunted for a week by the "twisties," a condition affecting spatial awareness, and concluded that it would not be safe for her or helpful to her team for her to continue to compete. In an Instagram post she described what she was experiencing this way—"It's honestly petrifying trying to do a skill but not having your mind and body in sync."

In a stunning move that captivated us all, she prioritized attending to her mental well-being, eventually coming back to win one bronze medal. Commenting on the rationale for her decision she said, "We're not just entertainment; we're humans. And there are things going on behind the scenes that we're also trying to juggle as well, on top of sports." Not only was she experiencing the stress of performing well, but she was also dealing with the aftereffects of going public about team doctor Larry Nassar's sexual abuse of the athletes under his care. As one of the young girls who had been abused, she was a leading voice in seeking to confront the systems that allowed this to happen and bring him to justice. This is the stuff of being human, and really, how much can one person take?

Biles did not come home with a fistful of gold medals, but standing on the podium with a bronze medal hanging around her neck, it was clear that twenty-four-year-old Biles had claimed something even more valuable—respect for her existence as a human being, not just a human doing. In reflecting later on this choice, she said, "It was something that was so out of my control, but the outcome I had at the end of the day, my mental and physical health is better than any medal."

Time will tell how history remembers her, but what do you think Simone Biles will be remembered for—the number of medals she earned in these particular Olympic games or the self-respect she demonstrated by acknowledging her limitations and prioritizing her long-term health and well-being over risking her life to perform in the expected ways? As past stories were recalled of young gymnasts who were paralyzed or in other ways gravely injured because they and those around them didn't know when to stop pushing, USA Gymnastics said in their statement, "We remain in awe of Simone, who continues to handle this situation with courage and grace." Awe, yes. We are in awe of a young woman who knows more about limits at twenty-four years old than many of us who are still pushing beyond limits rather than allowing them to inform our decisions in life-saving ways.

Sabbath shows us how to move beyond lamenting our limits as liabilities to embracing them as gifts that are part and parcel of being human—an aspect of our created selves that God actually intended and called good. This may be a new thought for

100

some of us. *My human limitations as a gift? Really? I'm so used to apologizing for my limitations and always trying to keep them under wraps!*

But what if the reality of limits really is part of how God created us that God pronounced good? What if important aspects of the will of God are contained within our limitations? What difference would it make if we believed this? And what would that mean in terms of how we might prioritize sabbath as a practice for helping us do exactly that? In his book *You're Only Human: How Your Limits Reflect God's Design and Why That's Good News*, Kelly Kapic offers these questions to help us reflect on our limitations as gifts and sources of insight about the human experience:

> What does it mean that we are creatures and not God? What does it mean that we have *these* talents and resources and not *all* talents and resources? What does it mean that we are finite, particular, and rooted, and not infinite, universal, or standing above all local circumstances? Answering these questions honestly will change how we imagine the world, ourselves, our relationship to God and others.

I could not agree more.

SAYING NO SO WE CAN SAY YES

The heart of God's intention for sabbath-keeping is that there would be this regular rhythm of ceasing our work for the purpose of resisting cultural influence and personal drivenness, so we can live on God's own terms for us. God knows we need a regular rhythm of rest, worship, and delight, so everything we choose to do and not do on sabbath should correspond to those categories. Sabbath is shaped by what we say no to, what we say yes to, and in what spirit. As we shape our sabbath time, there are several categories we would do well to exclude from our sabbath-keeping.

Work. It is important to be very thoughtful and discerning about what constitutes work for us and commit to not doing these things on the sabbath. This will take trial and error so never beat yourself up if, in your explorations, you try something that ended up feeling like work when you thought it was going to be restful and replenishing. And it will be helpful to identify the challenges and temptations related to your work specifically and your own tendencies so you can establish clear boundaries to protect sabbath time.

The greatest challenge for me in the beginning was having a home office, because it meant my work was easily accessible all the time. Since the Covid-19 pandemic there are more and more of us in this situation, and I have already told you about putting St. Francis in front of my office door! Another consequence of the advent of the computer and cellphone is that these devices allow us to work from anywhere, which has made it almost impossible to establish clear boundaries between work and home, work and family time, work and rest. The great temptation to check email, text messages, and social media (just once) or to try to get writing and speaking prep done (just a little) is a constant because the possibility is right there all the time.

As I struggled with my practice and experimented with "checking just once," I noticed that computers and communications technology carried me back into work mode and constant stimulation that is deadening to my spirit. The smartphone carries me back into constant connectivity, checking to be sure I haven't missed anything, with push notifications and news *coming at me* versus me having control over what I want to see and when, not to mention the rabbit holes they take me down. These things might serve a good purpose during the work week, but in the context of sabbath they are a real intrusion and do not help us enter into and maintain the restful posture we so desperately need.

We might also pay attention to whether or not a particular activity kicks up our activism, our addiction to productivity, or our feelings of indispensability. Yard work may be restful for some, but for others, it may be a way to check something off the to-do list, which is really not what sabbath is about. Real discernment of spirit is needed to recognize these inner dynamics and make sabbath decisions accordingly.

Buying and selling. On principle, if we are out buying, selling, and engaging in the world of commerce, we are feeding our consumerism, which is another aspect of life in our culture that needs a rest on the sabbath. The world of commerce functions to entice us into thinking we need things we don't really need and to convince us to buy things we can't really afford. It is a world designed to keep us overstimulated so we are never satisfied nor able to delight in the gifts of God that money cannot buy. To abstain from being a consumer one day a week sensitizes us to the more substantive gifts of God in our lives, fostering contentment instead of consumerism. This is another place where sabbath becomes a form of resistance because we are actively resisting a culture of consumption that grounds human value and identity in achievement and possession. In addition, if we refrain from buying and selling on the sabbath, we are not supporting the system that forces others to work on the sabbath.

Worry and emotional stress. There are more kinds of work than just physical work. There is also the emotional and mental hard work we engage in all week, trying to figure everything out in our lives and make it all work. Sabbath is an invitation to rest emotionally and mentally from engaging aspects of life that cause worry and stress—like taxes, budgets, to-do lists, event planning, major decision-making, conflict resolution, the twenty-four-hour news cycle, and so on. If we observe sabbath from Saturday evening to Sunday evening, perhaps Sunday evening after dinner is a time when, from a more rested place, we can engage the harder conversations and decision making that do need to be done, but just not when we are trying to rest. And we can also make plans for the next week so that we are not caught unprepared for Monday morning.

Technology. Given all we have discussed regarding technology, consider how you will limit or eliminate it as part of your sabbath practice. I do not want to tell you what to do about technology as much as I want to give you a way to think about technology—and that has to do with noticing what happens inside you with different kinds of technology. Here is how my good friend Bob Fryling has paid attention to this in his own life and practice:

> I take a defined break from electronic and commercial stimulation on the sabbath because I need to have a clean break from my weekday thoughts and activities. One particularly difficult choice for me was with respect to watching sports on television. Because I like to do so, I

used to think that watching a baseball or football game was a relaxing activity and sometimes it is—unless you are a Cubs fan! But when I was really honest with myself, I realized that often after a three-hour involvement with not only the game, but all the replays and the hyped up commentary, I was emotionally tired whether my team won or not. If they won I was excited and if they lost I was discouraged, but either way I was emotionally depleted. I was entertained but I was not rested.

I do not want to impose my disciplines on others, as we all need to sort out for ourselves what is restful and what is not. But even as a sports fan, I do think there is a level of idolatry and time consumption with sports that robs our souls of energy and spiritual vitality. Of course, there are idolatries for non-sports fans, like excessive shopping or movie watching that seem relaxing at first but can also weary our bodies and souls. The issue is not to be legalistic for each other but to be attentive to what is truly restful and provides the environment for a quiet heart.

SAYING YES TO REPLENISHMENT

So then, what is to replace all that we are excluding from our sabbath time? The simple answer is, whatever delights and replenishes you—body, mind, and soul. Here are some categories and ways of thinking about planning for replenishment.

Resting the body. What activities rest and replenish your body? The invitation of sabbath time is to replace the time you would normally spend working, shopping, and checking things off your to-do list with activities that rest and restore your physical self: wearing comfortable clothes, taking a nap, going for a walk or a bike ride, enjoying a hot shower or a long bubble bath just because it feels so good, eating your favorite foods (no dieting on the sabbath), sitting in the sun or lying in the grass, lighting candles, listening to beautiful music, making love. (As a side note, in Jewish tradition married couples get rabbinical brownie points for making love on the sabbath and double brownie points for making love twice. You've gotta' love a religion like that!)

Resting the mind, replenishing the spirit. Another sabbath invitation is to rest your hardworking mind and pay attention to what replenishes your spirit, choosing only those activities that delight you and bring you joy. Obviously, what falls in this category will be highly personal to each one of us, but it is the *most* amazing thing to have permission to get in touch with what delights you and to only do those things on this day, knowing God is in it. Pay close attention to activities that merely stimulate you or become filler and those that actually replenish you—in other words, those that leave you with more energy rather than feeling drained. Television and most things technological are not really replenishing; they are merely distractions from God's more meaningful gifts.

My favorite thing to do on the sabbath is so simple: I have a couch in my office that is really comfortable right in front of a sunny window facing a garden. I love to lie on that couch under a quilt (not a blanket but a quilt, because I love the weight and feel of them) and read a book for pleasure. On a really good sabbath I will get to do this for several hours. The couch itself is very comfortable and restful for my body and I savor how good that feels. Plus, I have many symbols and religious artifacts in my office that delight me and speak to me about God's presence with me. In fact, I have a bronze plaque hanging there that

106

simply says "Beloved" that my friend Vicki gave me, and on the sabbath I savor the fact that I am beloved—by her and by God! Since I love words but spend so much time working with words, reading for the sheer pleasure of it is the most delicious thing I could choose—novels, poetry, or a spiritual book for my own soul that I do not plan to share with others right away for any sort of ministry purpose. I also love it when different members of my family come into that space just to sit and talk quietly with me. There is rarely this kind of spaciousness during the work week and since it is so rare, it is one of the most precious things that ever happens to me. It replenishes me someplace deep inside.

Restoring the soul. The soul is the part of us that gets most lost during the work week, which is governed almost completely by the value of productivity. Perhaps the deepest refreshment is the invitation to renew your soul by *being with God with what is*, trusting God to keep working even while you're resting, and engaging the life-giving presence of God through prayer, worship, and quiet reflection. Of course, you will want to incorporate worship with your faith community, but you may also find it replenishing to incorporate more personal ways of lifting your soul to God. As an individual you might be able to spend some extra time in silence and prayer, take a slow, meditative walk, or read a spiritual book God has been using in your life and then journal about it. You might also do an extended version of the *examen,* looking back over your whole week to notice where God was present, where God felt absent, where God was at work transforming you (praise God!), and where you might have been caught in a place of un-freedom and you need to confess something to God. You may want to give particular attention to those things you are grateful for (which will lead to private worship) or an experience or a Scripture from the past week that caught your attention because God seemed to have something to say in and through it. It is an amazing thing to have space to listen, ponder, and make meaning.

As a family (if children are old enough), consider maintaining a quieter and more spacious feeling in your home for at least part of the day. Pay attention to how you can express love to each other on this day. Identify rituals or shared activities that create a spirit of reverence for God and enjoyment of each other. Share a special meal preceded by the lighting of candles and a Scripture reading. Over dinner go around the table and share where God seemed particularly present with you during the week. Turn off the TV and talk with each other. Take a walk together, play games, write or call long-distance loved ones. Open your home to friends, family, or neighbors.

A FLOATING SABBATH?

Invariably when the topic of sabbath comes around, someone will ask, "Is it okay to have a 'floating sabbath'?" This is a question that warrants care and great sensitivity because some professions (the medical profession, restaurant workers, retail sales, etc.) require floating the sabbath to different days of the week or month because schedules change regularly. I do not want to tend at all toward legalism, and this is a place where Jesus' statement, "The sabbath was made for humankind, and not humankind for the sabbath" (Mark 2:27), really does apply. Since Jesus is Lord of the sabbath *and* the sabbath is made for us in whatever vocational situation we find ourselves in, Jesus can guide us in intimate ways toward solutions that honor God and honor our human needs. That said, establishing a regular rhythm of sabbath-keeping is important if there is any way at all to swing it. And here's why.

As we observed earlier, human bodies and souls respond well to regular rhythms and, in fact, are accustomed to living in seasonal rhythms and daily rhythms. Part of the delight and restful feeling of sabbath is knowing that it is always coming in consistent intervals so we're not having to make decisions about it every week. When sabbath is observed on different days every week, we actually add a stressor to our lives— figuring out week by week when the sabbath is going to be. If we are practicing as a family, we might have to call a family summit every time it comes to planning our sabbath!

A floating sabbath also means there will be weeks when we go longer than seven days without rest and the needed break from the intensity and pressure of work and life in our culture; we risk drifting into dangerous levels of exhaustion and an inner life that is a pressure cooker ready to blow. Wayne Muller drives this point home:

> Because we do not rest we lose our way. We miss the compass points that would show us where to go, we bypass the nourishment that would give us succor. We miss the quiet that would give us wisdom. We miss the joy and love born of effortless delight. Poisoned by the hypnotic belief that good things come only through unceasing determination and tireless effort, we can never truly rest. And for want of rest our lives are in danger.

Grace abounds for situations that do not allow for regularity, and God can find us and replenish us even if we can't establish regular sabbath patterns. But as you think about incorporating sabbath into your life, if at all possible, try to establish a regular rhythm. You'll be glad you did!

BEGINNINGS AND ENDINGS

Beginnings and endings matter, so if there is any way you can have a clear beginning to sabbath and a clear ending, that would be most helpful—for your own psyche and for your shared experience with others. For the Hebrews, sabbath began on Friday night with the lighting of candles and a special meal. For many of us, sabbath would likely begin on Saturday night, extending into Sunday, and this is a great way to begin if you can make it work. I love the way Wayne Muller describes a beginning ritual: "Light a candle, alone or with friends. Let each of you speak about those things that are left to do, and as the candle burns, allow the cares to melt away. Do not be anxious about tomorrow, said Jesus. The worries of today are sufficient for today. Whatever remains to be done, for now, let it be."

Given my history, I do have concern about how much of the work of preparing for the sabbath might fall to the women of the house, making sabbath something less than restful for them. We need to be careful about this and make sure everyone shares in the work of preparing. For sabbath to work for everyone, the whole family needs to help. Do not let the table setting, the shopping, and the cleanup fall to one person. Consider going out sometimes if preparations don't get made in time. Meals could be more simple with food that has been bought and mostly prepared before sabbath begins. For families who enjoy cooking together, preparing food could be a wonderful way of spending time together—one person grilling the steaks, someone else chopping vegetables, and others helping set the table. Even though it might seem easier to do everything yourself, in the more relaxed environment of sabbath, involve young children who really enjoy the feeling of importance that comes from feeling like they have contributed. Or in a family with older children, have everyone contribute a specialty or a recipe they want to try. You could also make your special meal the dinner at the end of sabbath when everyone is rested and ready to enjoy the process of preparing and cooking together.

One of the best things we did with our family during the teen years was to make sure dinner on the sabbath was fantastic—with special foods we didn't usually buy and recipes we didn't usually make. Even if nothing else went quite right for our sabbath plans, knowing dinner would be extra-special pretty much guaranteed people found a way to be present for what oftentimes felt like a celebration.

"DO SOMETHING BEFORE YOU DO EVERYTHING"

This is one piece of advice I have found helpful in a multitude of situations, and it is in that spirit that I make this recommendation: determine that you will try *one* sabbath. Don't feel like you have to change your whole life—yet. Look out over the next six months on your calendar and pick *one day* that would work for you (and anyone you want to practice with) to set aside as your sabbath. (See appendix A for a worksheet that will help you shape your sabbath time.) Have faith that the God who calls you is faithful, and God will do it, no matter how impossible it may feel on a human level or how countercultural it is. If no one else in your life is ready to try it with you, determine that you will try it for yourself. The only person you can control is you—and who knows what might happen if you follow God in this way?

What Your Soul Wants to Say to God

Take some time to reflect on the questions raised in this chapter in a very personal way.

- *What does it mean to you that you are a creature, you are not God? How and when are you most in touch with this reality?*

- *How do you relate to the idea of limits? Do you tend to lament your limits, ignore them, hide them, overcome them, use them as excuses? What would it be like to embrace limits as part of God's goodness in creating you? Let yourself imagine it.*

- *Be specific in listing some of the gifts and talents you do have and a few that you don't. Following up on the questions offered by Kelly Kapic in this chapter: What does it mean that you have these talents and resources and not all talents and resources? How might embracing the gifts you do have and accepting the limits of what you don't have be freeing for you?*

- *What does it mean that you are "finite, particular, and rooted" in a particular life and set of circumstances rather than being infinite, universal, or standing above all local circumstances? How might sabbath-keeping help you to stay rooted and grounded in the particularities of your life rather than standing apart from your life?*

Then listen to your own longings regarding the sabbath. Where were the places in your reading that resonated deeply and touched your own desire for the rhythms and practices of sabbath? Let yourself feel how deep your desire goes and allow it to guide you, believing this is a true desire of the heart God wants to meet (Psalm 37:4). (If you already have a sabbath practice in place, reflect on how it's going and if there are any adjustments you would like to make based on what you have read.)

Where did you feel resistance or feelings of impossibility welling up—especially in your life as a leader? What do you feel most drawn to try? Sit quietly with your own longings and any issues these raise for you. In Deuteronomy 30:15-19, God says, "I have set before you today life and prosperity, death and adversity. . . . Choose life so that you and your descendants may live." Ask God to help you choose life.

Interlude

ON TIME

RUTH HALEY BARTON

● ● ●

There have to be times in your life when you move slow,
    times when you walk rather than run, settling into each step . . .
There have to be times when you stop and gaze admiringly at
        loved ones,
    marveling that they have been given to you for this life . . .
times when hugs linger and kisses are real,
    when food and drink are savored with gratitude and humility
        rather than gulped down on your way to something else.
There have to be times when you read for the sheer pleasure of it,
    marveling at the beauty of words
        and the endless creativity in putting them together . . .
times when you settle into the comforts of home
        and become human once again.
There have to be times when you light a candle and
    find the tender place inside you that loves or sorrows or sings
        and you pray from that place,
times when you let yourself *feel*, when you allow the tears to come
    rather than blinking them back because you don't have time to cry.
There have to be times to sink into the soft body of yourself
    and love what you love simply because love itself is a grace . . .
times when you sit with gratitude for the good gifts of your life
    that get lost and forgotten in the rush of things . . .

times to celebrate and play
to roll down hills
to splash in water or make leaf piles
to spread paint on paper or walls or each other.
There have to be times to sit and wait for the fullness of God
that replenishes body, mind, and soul—
if you can even stand to be so full.
There has to be time
for the fullness of time
or time is meaningless.

9

LEADING *a*
SABBATH COMMUNITY

● ● ●

The church's primary social and psychological task is to help
people manage their experienced dependency upon God in
such a way that they are better able to care effectively for
the world. These two dimensions of dependency and caring
define the needed human rhythm of life. The church is the
only large-scale institution in society that is accountable
for and capable of fostering such an authentic rhythm.

TILDEN EDWARDS

DAN HAD BEEN A PASTOR for twenty years in a contemporary-
model church focused on drawing seekers into a life of devotion
to Christ while also engaging the needs in their neighborhood.
The church is located in an urban environment in a major city,
and its reach encompasses upscale housing inhabited by young
professionals as well as neighborhoods where people struggle
for economic survival and gun violence encroaches on the lives

of families who attend the church. Issues such as racial injustice and inequity coupled with political divisiveness started to intensify, and the pressure to understand and address these issues meaningfully as part of the community's life together was mounting. Seminary had not prepared Dan for this.

When Dan was being honest, he was aware of a level of exhaustion that was not the result of one crisis or intense season of ministry; rather, his exhaustion had accumulated over years of functioning beyond limits, stuffing the inevitable pains of life in ministry, soldiering on, and putting a brave face on things. His normal breaks and vacations were really good times with his family and provided welcome opportunities for him to fish, hike, and travel, which he loved, but they did not fully replenish the deeper exhaustion he felt.

On the surface he was managing fairly well, but he was aware that he was on the edge of what his skills, competencies, and seminary training prepared him for. Leadership books and conferences provided momentary inspiration, but they were not giving him the profound wisdom and insight he needed. The deepest truth of all is that he was missing a more intimate connection with God in the depths of his own soul. Beyond all the spiritual experiences he was working so hard to create for others, he had deep spiritual longings that he didn't know how to pay attention to. He could barely admit these things to himself, let alone figure out what to do with them. There was a deep soul weariness that had set in.

At the same time, he was very concerned about his church—especially his staff and high-level volunteers. Although he was proud of the fact that his church was viewed as being very cool and current, he knew he had probably been asking too much of people for way too long. In fact, some of the people that had been most committed over the years—people he would consider to be his friends—had simply left because they couldn't keep up the pace of working jobs, raising children, and volunteering in all sorts of ways at the church. Sometimes they were considerate enough to schedule a meeting and tell him in person about the fact that they were leaving; other times they simply melted away. Either way, it hurt, and sometimes Dan wished *he* had the freedom to melt away in order to seek out a way of life that would work better for *him*. He knew he was on an edge and that those who served alongside him were too.

And then he made a connection with a young couple who had visited a few times and even attended a membership class. They were the kind of couple that makes an impression—exuding leadership and spiritual promise. He noticed that he found himself looking for them as he preached, and when he didn't see them after a few weeks he followed up with a phone call to ask where they were and what they were thinking. They were polite in their willingness to schedule a phone call, and when they finally connected, they were very clear that one of their highest priorities was finding a church community that would support them in maintaining a sustainable lifestyle—a way of life in God that would be life-giving for them and their growing family. They described seasons of being busy and almost consumed by being involved in a church, and they were not looking to do that again. They needed Sunday to be a day of rest and regrouping as a family, and so far they had not found a church that was structured to help with this. So their answer to Dan's church was, "Thanks, but no thanks."

Dan was disappointed but he couldn't disagree with their reasoning. If fact, if he hadn't been the pastor, he might have seriously considered the same thing himself!

PUTTING ON YOUR OWN OXYGEN MASK FIRST

These days pastors and parishioners alike are looking for a way of life that works. In fact, many would say it is their deepest need and desire—or at least the one they are most aware of. As Tilden Edwards stated in the quote at the beginning of this chapter, the church is uniquely positioned to help with this and in fact it is the *only* large-scale institution that can. Except, it's not.

Fortunately, Dan was starting to pay attention to all the issues that were converging in this moment and he realized that he could not continue to soldier on as usual; this was one disappointment too many. Rather than trying to convince himself he was okay, it was time for him to stop and reflect deeply on his life and leadership, in that order.

First of all, he sought out a spiritual director who could provide a safe place for him to be truly honest about the exhaustion he was getting in touch with. He was surprised by how deep the tiredness went and how many levels and layers there were. He was surprised at how close he felt to quitting. He was surprised by his feelings of powerlessness. He was surprised by the tears that came sometimes when the tender places within him were touched.

After listening together for a while, Dan's spiritual director asked him about his practice of sabbath and together they uncovered the fact that Dan really did not have an effective sabbath practice. He did take the balance of Sundays following morning church services as time off, but mostly he got home around one o'clock famished and exhausted and just collapsed on the couch, too tired to enjoy anything. Together they noticed that because he was so spent from pouring out in two church services, he often chose escapist, numbing behaviors (like vegging out in front of the TV or bingeing on Netflix) rather than napping and doing other things that would be truly replenishing. Then on Sunday evenings when he had regained a little energy, he would check email and start getting ready for Monday so he could hit the ground running. Not only was he *not* fully unplugging and engaging in activities that were truly replenishing, but his sabbath simply wasn't long enough.

Paying attention to this pattern helped Dan realize that he had never really considered the importance of a full twenty-four-hour sabbath because he had assumed he needed to be back at it right away on Mondays. After all, they needed to debrief the Sunday services and start getting ready for the next week, right? Dan and his spiritual director further identified that even though he had been taking Fridays as a "sabbath," that is not really what it was. It was really a day for doing errands and human tasks—which were all needed—but it was the furthest thing from a day of rest.

In discernment with his spiritual director, Dan began to work on a more intentional approach to sabbath-keeping in his personal life, keeping it somewhat private so he would have greater freedom to explore rather than making pronouncements too early or opening himself to resistance he was not yet ready to handle. To start with, he determined he would take Sundays from the end of church services all the way through the evening on Monday—a little more than twenty-four hours.

He communicated this on a need-to-know basis with his assistant, fellow staff members, and the board of elders and found them all to be supportive. There were stops and starts, sabbaths that went well and sabbaths that provided valuable learning; with the support of his spiritual director and the resources she recommended, slowly he found himself coming back from the brink of dangerous exhaustion.

This was Dan's first and most important step in leading a sabbath community.

SHARING WITH HIS LEADERSHIP COMMUNITY

Eventually Dan felt confident enough about his sabbath experience to share it more fully with others. He asked for time during one of the upcoming board meetings to share the dangerous place he had found himself in, the way he had been drawn into sabbath-keeping, and the resources that were supporting him. He even shared a bit of his understanding of Scripture on this point, hoping to inspire others with the idea that sabbath is not simply a lifestyle suggestion but is actually a command given to us for our good. He invited their questions and comments and even their own personal sharing about their view of sabbath, and was surprised at how intimate the meeting became. Because Dan had shared so openly about his own exhaustion and sense of concern for himself and their church, others felt free to do the same; they acknowledged their own tiredness and doubts about whether they were guiding their community into a life-giving way of life or whether they were just wearing people out. They began to sense that it was part of their spiritual leadership to keep asking these questions and see where it would all lead.

There was one rather hard-driving business person in the meeting who expressed some resistance and concern about whether they were all getting a little soft, and whether they would be able to meet their church growth goals if people started hearing about sabbath. But because of Dan's quiet confidence about the spiritual and biblical nature of sabbath and the clear difference it was making in his life, this person settled down pretty quickly.

What happened next surprised Dan even more—several of the elders expressed their desire to explore this further, asking if they could take half an hour at the beginning of future meetings for Dan to lead them in teachings and discussions about sabbath-keeping. Dan readily agreed, and thus began their sabbath journey in community.

As they began to explore and discuss the practice of sabbath, it didn't take long for other members of the group to feel drawn to figuring out a sabbath practice for themselves; they looked forward to discussing their experiences, wrestling with the knotty issues sabbath-keeping raised, and sharing ideas with one another. Of course, those who worked more traditional jobs had different situations than Dan, given the fact that his work life culminated on Sundays rather than being oriented around the Monday–Friday work week. But having a group to brainstorm with felt like a blessing to everyone in the group; all in all it was very inspiring.

Eventually Dan felt led to start working in the very same way with the staff, to see if they could also incorporate sabbath more intentionally into their life rhythms. Once again, he began by being vulnerable about the dangerous place he had found himself in, the work he had been doing with a spiritual director, what he was learning about sabbath-keeping, and how it felt like sabbath was saving his life. He also shared his concern for the staff and the volunteers they supervised—and his desire that they might be able to find a way of life that worked as well. As he looked around the table, he noticed there were tears in people's eyes, and it seemed to have to do with the vulnerability in what he was sharing about himself, and also the tenderness of his care and concern for them.

There was great readiness and openness from the staff to start a process similar to what the elders had been going through. All of a sudden their church felt like a pretty good place to work!

SHEPHERDING THE FLOCK

The staff and the elders leaned in to their sabbath practice; they worked out the details of taking their sabbath time on Mondays so they could all roll from Sunday services into sabbath and get a full twenty-four hours. They considered staggering their sabbaths so different staff members would take different days but realized there was a difference in being unplugged and resting when others were also unplugged versus knowing that while they were resting, others were working and filling up their inboxes. They had a strong sense that there was something about the whole community resting together on the same day that would be good for everyone.

They worked it out for the church to be closed the rest of the day after services on Sunday (no additional meetings or gatherings), and they hired a part-time receptionist to answer the phones on Mondays with an assigned pastor on call to handle emergencies. Pastors *and* elders took turns being on call so that they needed to be available only once every two months.

Once the staff and the elders had been working on their own sabbath practice for a while, it didn't take long for them to start feeling so passionate about the goodness they were experiencing that they wanted to share it with the congregation as a whole. There was a strong sense that there was a role for them to play in introducing people to this life-giving way, and that this was an important part of their spiritual leadership.

They spent time planning how they would introduce a sabbath practice to the congregation—starting with a preaching series Dan would offer, followed by adult Sunday school classes and community group gatherings throughout the following month to offer ample opportunity to process the teaching and make practical applications. They developed a discussion guide to help with these conversations and also handpicked a few published resources to provide further guidance for making practical decisions. They scheduled the community groups in such a way that participants had time to go home and try things and then come back to debrief before moving on. In some cases, they created groups made up of people in similar life stages so they could share ideas. It was all very exciting.

The culmination of all this was a date six months in the future when the whole congregation would take a sabbath together, putting into practice the plans they had made. There was a great deal of excitement about the idea of doing it once before trying to change their whole lives. This felt doable.

A PRACTICE THAT WILL MESS
WITH YOUR COMMUNITY

At the same time, the staff's shared attempts at sabbath-keeping were creating some uncomfortable moments. One of those moments came when they were having a strategic planning meeting about whether or not to add a Saturday night service to the two services they already held on Sundays. Both of those services were 80 percent full, and they were aware of church growth wisdom indicating that at that point new people will not come because they feel there isn't room for them. Strategically, it made all the sense in the world to introduce a Saturday evening service—until one of the practically minded administrative staff brought up the question about what this would mean for their newly minted sabbath practice.

There was a series of questions that emerged at this point: What would it mean for the worship team, Sunday school teachers, and other volunteers who worked a full week at their jobs to have to be at the church for an even more significant chunk of their weekend? How would *they* ever get a sabbath and how then would the staff ever be able to lead them in this life-giving practice? And what about "the sixth day"—the day that needs to be set aside for the work of being human? If the seventh day was going to work at all, when would staff get their "sixth day" if they had to be at church on Saturdays too?

There was dead silence.

At first Dan felt awkward, because he had come into this meeting really wanting to move toward adding a third service. Even though he had not yet been fully aware of it, adding this service was for him a symbol that things were going well, a signal of his success as a pastor—in addition to the ministry impact, of course! So at first he got a little defensive and tried brainstorming ways it could work; what followed was a very robust conversation in which many ideas were discussed. But eventually the conversation came around to "the question beneath the question": How much did they actually value their sabbath practice? Some wanted to press forward with strategies for numerical growth while others were convinced they should nail down this practice in the community's life before adding anything else to the schedule.

As uncomfortable as this moment was, it became a defining moment for the group, because they had to grapple with how deep their commitment to sabbath really went.

WHAT'S GOING ON?

When churches hesitate or out-and-out resist cultivating a sabbath way of life I always feel curious and wonder what is really going on. First of all, I wonder if we really see sabbath as the God-ordained rhythm that it is, designed intentionally for our well-being and the well-being of all. We might see it as a duty, an obligation, a luxury, a drudgery, a nice option, an interruption, or even a holdover from a past life, but not as a gift we are invited to open and enjoy today, let alone a commandment that is meant to hold society together.

But there is a darker possibility as well, and that is that many communities simply don't want their priorities, their schedules, and their growth plans to be messed with. They've set visions, goals, and strategies that always seem to require more—more programming, more ministry, more financial and numerical growth—and packing Sundays with church-related activities seems like the only way to get it all done.

I also suspect there is a certain level of fear that if we don't grab people on Sundays when they're already there, we'll never get them back! I am not saying that sabbath always has to be kept on Sundays, but for many families Sunday is the only day when practicing sabbath is even possible. For that reason, we need to consider the day itself very carefully because if a good portion of a community can keep sabbath the same day, it will be supportive of everyone who is attempting this challenging discipline.

This is one of the many reasons sabbath-keeping needs to be *led* by senior leaders and *supported* by a practicing community—because sabbath-keeping will mess with us, not just as individuals but as a group! It will mess with our priorities, our scheduling, and even our sacred cows. Guiding a group of people into embracing a sabbath life together takes vision (what it could be) and conviction (*why* it should be), along with consistent, faith-filled leadership. By that I mean the ongoing presence of leaders who are practicing sabbath themselves and who are utterly convinced this is the life-giving rhythm God intends for them. For this reason, they have no problem ordering their community's life around it.

Fortunately, Dan was that kind of leader. Because he was growing in self-awareness through the attention he was now giving to his inner life, he recognized that the questions being raised about a Saturday evening service were really important and warranted more time and space for discernment. He felt pretty sure that the defensiveness he was feeling was coming from ego rather than spiritual wisdom and insight, and he wanted to get with God to see what was going on there. So after a robust discussion in which many ideas were presented, he suggested they slow down and take some time for prayer and further reflection. He cast vision for them to continue the process of solidifying the communal aspects of their sabbath practice and made the commitment that they would revisit the question of adding a third service at a later time.

In the meantime, they all agreed, Dan would prepare and deliver a six-week sermon series on sabbath rest and also provide multiple opportunities for people to engage in group discussions following each sermon. These discussions were designed to help people get really practical about building sane rhythms of work and rest into their lives while also providing ongoing support.

COMING BACK TO LIFE

Dan started the series by sharing in a very open and vulnerable way the dangerous levels of exhaustion he had experienced, and how through spiritual direction and other resources, he had been incorporating sabbath rhythms into his life. He shared how God was using sabbath to bring him back to life, helping him to experience God's goodness once again.

With love and tenderness—the kind that can only come from the heart of a shepherd—he told the congregation that he was committed to sharing with them the goodness of what he had been receiving through the gift of sabbath, and he expressed his heartfelt desire that they would become a community that ordered its life around shared sabbath rhythms. He described the process he and the elders and staff had been engaged in together and affirmed that they were unified in their commitment to this way of life—to the extent that they had agreed they would not add any more ministries or activities until this value and practice was embedded in their community's life. He knew that eventually they would talk about offering sabbaticals to their leaders as another aspect of becoming a sabbath community, but for now this felt like enough.

To Dan's surprise, after the last word of that sermon was spoken, the congregation rose to their feet in a spontaneous standing ovation. This had never happened before and he was completely taken by surprise. It was like a wave of unity was sweeping through their community and just for a moment causing lines of divisiveness and difference to recede. Amid all the issues that were swirling, the desire to discover a way of life that worked was something they all wanted and could all agree on. It transcended so many of their differences. And the idea that they might do it together and support one another and help each other? That was almost too good to be true.

As Dan looked into the faces of the dear sheep God had given him to shepherd—some with tears shining in their eyes—he felt his love for them for the first time in a long while. He saw that his desire for a way of life that worked matched their own. He saw that his longing for sabbath rest matched their longing for sabbath rest. *And* he saw their gratitude that God had given them a good shepherd—one who was committed to leading them beside still waters so their souls could be restored regularly in God's presence.

Dan was in his sweet spot again—shepherding his flock in rhythms of dependency on God. He knew that whatever issues were before them, they would face them together from a more rested, alert, and trusting place guided by their Great Shepherd whose promises hold true today just like they held true so many years ago.

● ● ●

KEY MOVEMENTS IN CULTIVATING
A SABBATH COMMUNITY

Following are the key movements in leading a sabbath community as illustrated in Pastor Dan's story. As you reflect on these movements, consider where you are in the process and how God might be guiding you to take next steps.

Establish your own practice of sabbath-keeping. There is no substitute for the inner authority that comes from your own mature practice of sabbath-keeping. I suggest you have at least six months to a year of substantive practice under your belt before you begin teaching, leading, and advising others. While there will be many who support what you are trying to do, you may also get resistance when you first introduce these concepts and related practices with all their implications. The solid conviction that comes from knowing how important and necessary this is *for you* will give you a calm presence as you teach and lead. You may need to bolster your resolve by continuing to read and reflect on sabbath.

Share with those who lead with you. Begin sharing with your board, elders, vestry, staff (whoever leads with you) your conviction about how valuable sabbath-keeping is to you and your desire to share this goodness with others in your community. Begin sharing the vision you have for ordering your community's life together more intentionally around sabbath-keeping. Read and discuss this book together (see "Becoming a Sabbath Community: A Conversation Guide for Groups" after the appendixes) or choose other resources you think would be helpful and supportive of your group's process. Keep your language invitational rather than dictatorial or top down. Give others the chance to fall in love with sabbath, sharing your learnings and experiences together in very intimate ways for a while.

Seek agreement about incorporating sabbath into your life together. After your leadership group has been practicing for a while and the moment seems right (timing is everything), discuss whether or not there is a shared conviction regarding sabbath-keeping you as leaders are ready to lead out on in your community. Becoming a sabbath community involves believing sabbath is a gift from God and that it is a Christian discipline you want to embrace together. It is an important part of guiding your community into a way of life that works rather than settling for a life of Christian busyness.

There are no emergencies with God, so take whatever time you need to discern and agree on this value together. Discuss any changes that need to be made in the community's schedule and priorities in order to make the introduction of this value and practice possible—including tackling honestly any sacred cows you might be aware of.

Cast vision. Once you as leaders have come to unity on how you want to lead your community, use whatever means you have—preaching, teaching, small groups, Christian education settings—(1) to help people get in touch with their desire for sane rhythms of work and rest, (2) to teach and cast vision for the biblical and theological basis for sabbath as a communal practice, and (3) to get really practical about how this might work for individuals and in your life together. Do not make heavy-handed pronouncements, but invite people by saying, "This is what we're going to try; would you like to join us?" Be careful not to make judgments but create safe spaces for discussing knotty issues like workplace scheduling, bosses who insist that employees be available 24-7, sports, technology, and meetings and activities that are already scheduled on Sundays.

Set aside a day in the future when you will all take a sabbath together. Similar to what you have tried on your own, plan for a day far enough in the future that your whole community can take a sabbath together. If it is going to be on a Sunday, plan to worship together on Saturday night or Sunday morning and then release everyone to their plans for sabbath. To help everyone prepare, schedule smaller group conversations where people in similar life stages can brainstorm together how it might work for them. Categories might include college students, single folks, newly marrieds, couples with young children, families with teenagers, empty-nesters, and the elderly who are living alone or in retirement communities. If possible, have someone in that life stage with sabbath-keeping experience lead and facilitate the conversation.

It goes without saying that all staff will participate, so make plans to have a pastor or Stephen minister on call, or a receptionist who can respond to any emergencies that arise. Over time, this responsibility can be shared in such a way that no one misses out consistently on sabbath.

Debrief and determine a way forward. After your sabbath experiment, schedule a time to debrief people's experiences, answer questions, and begin envisioning a way forward. Hopefully this one experience is so positive that the community eventually decides they want to establish sabbath as a regular pattern in their life together. I strongly suggest that everyone, including church staff, attempt to take the same day or that there is significant overlap. While those who are not on staff can perhaps take their sabbath from Saturday evening to Sunday evening, church staff and volunteers who are involved in carrying out worship services and Sunday morning ministries can take Sunday after church until Monday at noon or through the evening. When possible, plan for all staff to take the same day as their sabbath.

Consider scheduling decisions in light of your sabbath rhythms. Moving forward, make scheduling decisions with consideration for how they will affect the community's commitment to sabbath. Consider specific scheduling issues that make sabbath-keeping difficult or impossible. For instance, will any meetings other than worship be scheduled on Sundays if that is the day you have identified as the community's sabbath? Each and every time you add a new program, service, or ministry initiative, include the sabbath as a routine part of the discussion; determine to support your commitment to sabbath in every decision you make. Be patient. This may be challenging and it will take time, but commit your way to the Lord; trust in him, and he will act (Psalm 37:5).

Discuss the quote from Tilden Edwards at the beginning of this chapter. Do you agree or disagree?

How do you respond to the idea of moving beyond sabbath as a private discipline to leading and cultivating a sabbath community? Do you experience this as part of your calling? Take as much time as you need to speak to God about this.

If you do sense this as part of your calling and as you feel ready, reflect on some of the key movements in cultivating such a community as they were illustrated in this chapter and outlined on pages 130-134; identify where you are in the flow of the following movements and where you feel called to go next.

Part Two

SABBATICAL

10

WHEN SABBATH IS
NOT ENOUGH

● ● ●

*A sabbatical is an extension of weekly Sabbath rest. Taking leave
to build up or renew your spirit may prevent you from leaving
the ministry altogether before it's God's time for you to do so.*

DAVID ALVES

WHEN I WAS GIVEN THE GIFT of my first sabbatical, I was
beyond exhausted and not embarrassed to admit it. The organization I had founded and led since its inception had been
through its hardest season ever, a financial crisis in which we
almost lost everything for which we had worked so hard for over
fifteen years. Most of the year leading up to my sabbatical had
been spent making the kinds of choices no leader ever wants to
make—selling our property, letting cherished coworkers and
long-held dreams slip through my fingers, while doing all I
could to pour love and prayers over every letting go. I was bat-
tered, bruised, and spent. A puff of smoke. Toast.

At the same time, I was coming off several years of being geographically close to and providing care for my parents who were sick and aging. My mom had died two and half years earlier after a slow decline from a blood disorder that eventually turned into leukemia. My dad never really adjusted to his new reality, so he was alone, in need of care on every level, and beginning his own decline. He passed away in the April preceding my summer sabbatical from a general failure to thrive, even though we had done everything we could to help him thrive. All in all, it had been five years of providing intense loving care for my parents while at the same time managing the escalating demands of leadership in the midst of crisis.

These harsher realities were juxtaposed with the happy reality of our daughters and their families growing by leaps and bounds with the rapid addition of precious grandchildren. I longed to be fully present to the gifts of my growing family, but instead every day was full of constant juggling—what was needed for my ministry to survive, what my parents needed, what I longed to give my family, and what I needed as a finite human being. All the while my deepest vocation—the calling to write—kept getting pushed to the back burner, so there was an undercurrent of sadness and longing that flowed silently under the surface of my life. Every day was an experience of being pulled to pieces by hard choices and competing priorities—never feeling like I could do enough or be enough. I was crushed by the awareness that I was always inconveniencing or disappointing someone—including myself.

It's not like we hadn't tried to arrange for a sabbatical sooner. We had, several times. But the combination of crisis and care just had not made it possible. I was long overdue.

140

NO PERFECT TIME

Why am I telling you all this? To let you know that there is never a perfect time to take a sabbatical. There is either an impossible time or a slightly better time. The previous year really *had* been impossible, and this year was only slightly better; but we took it.

I am telling you this to alert you to the fact that sabbatical never comes easy; it will always need to be fought for. And I am intentionally drawing attention to the fact that often it's the *combination* of our leadership responsibilities plus what's going on in our personal lives that brings leaders to the point where sabbath-keeping begins to fall short of the kind of rest needed to prevent dangerous levels of exhaustion. Leaders are human, too, but somehow accumulating levels of exhaustion are lost to our awareness and we fail to recognize the toll it is taking. I also wonder if we are *afraid* to notice because we're not sure what we will do if we acknowledge what's really going on. But as leaders, we simply must pay attention to our humanity and our human limitations. This is called self-responsibility or self-leadership—which, by all counts, is the most challenging leadership task of all.

What was most uncomfortable for me to acknowledge in all this is that I had been deeply committed to a weekly sabbath for years, and yet here I was needing to admit that it wasn't enough. I had reached a level of exhaustion that a regular pattern of sabbath-keeping could not touch. Although I had written, taught, and preached that sabbath-keeping is the kingpin of a life well-lived in God, more often than not I would get to the end of Sunday (my sabbath) and a feeling of dread and panic would set in because I knew I was nowhere near fully rested.

As I faced each new work week, I longed to feel rested and ready, but I simply was not. Most Mondays I showed up for what was needed while painfully aware that I was just soldiering on, praying I could make it, hoping I could be all that my life required. I knew the people around me could see how frayed around the edges I was; it was just plain embarrassing to have one's humanity hanging out there for all to see. I longed for more rest than a weekly sabbath could provide but didn't know how to get it.

As my dad was laid to rest and our organization completed a series of hard choices in our attempt to survive our financial crisis, the Covid-19 pandemic hit. While there were many horrible losses our world endured during this crisis, one good hard thing that happened is that we were forced to cancel all in-person events. And that's when we saw the opening—just a few weeks out—for me to take my illusive sabbatical and for our whole organization to enter into a season of dormancy. We recognized that just like soil, we needed to lie fallow, to heal, to receive rather than give. It was time for us to receive care rather than continuing to give out, to carefully nurture and cultivate our bodies, minds, and spirits— weeding out what was choking the good growth in our souls and taking in the sweet nourishment God was waiting to give.

While I wouldn't recommend planning a sabbatical in a matter of weeks, it's what we had, and we determined to make the best of it. I poured out my desire and need into a proposal, which our board approved and then championed. We were honest with our supporters about what we needed, and they helped us achieve this rhythm that was so long overdue, supporting us immediately with gifts to fund the additional expenses associated with this time. Our staff came together to figure out how things would run while I was away, and I simply left. While our planning was not perfect, we made sabbatical happen, and that's all that mattered.

OF OR PERTAINING TO THE SABBATH

Imagine my delight when, as a sabbath-lover, I discovered that sabbatical literally means "of or pertaining to the Sabbath." I had heard about people taking sabbaticals to write books and do research projects, but according to *Clergy Renewal: The Alban Guide to Sabbatical Planning,*

> the essence of Sabbatical is rooted in the Hebrew word *sabbat* and the biblical traditions surrounding it. The first practice is that of the Sabbath day described in the creation story of Genesis 1 and 2: God rested on the seventh day from all the work he had done. . . . The second sabbatical practice is allowing the land to lie fallow every seventh year, as prescribed in Leviticus 25:3-4. . . . The third sabbatical practice is that of the Jubilee Year (Leviticus 25:8-13) in which every fiftieth year is used for celebration with no harvest, produce or rent, but with debt forgiveness and the making of offerings instead.

It was only more recently that sabbatical become associated with academia as an opportunity for professors to pursue further achievement—that is, a time away from the relentless demands of classroom responsibilities in order to write for publication, research an important topic in their chosen field, or take on a project that requires one's complete focus.

A case in point: while on sabbatical, the monthly publication from my alma mater arrived in my mailbox and it contained a section called "Faculty Sabbatical Notes." Intrigued to see what others were experiencing on their sabbaticals, imagine my shock when *all of the notes* had to do with projects different professors had worked on during their sabbaticals. No one said anything about rest; no, not one.

"During my sabbatical I made substantial progress on my book project . . ."

"I spent much of my sabbatical preparing a special recital . . ."

"In addition to continuing research on a book project about . . . , I partnered with [so-and-so] to research and write a report . . ."

"I am using linked historical US census data to examine . . ."

"During sabbatical, I wrote several essays . . ."

For a moment I wobbled, feeling like a total slacker for not having any such goals or projects planned for my sabbatical. *Didn't anyone else need rest from their overachieving ways?* I wondered. If we don't use sabbatical times for deeper levels of rest, when will we ever get it?

Don't get me wrong—every project described in these faculty notes was very valuable and I'm sure the world is a better place because of them; however, I did find myself wishing they had used different language to name this opportunity. There is an important and wonderful place for the academic model of sabbatical, but it is decidedly different from the biblical and spiritual concept of sabbatical as a time for rest and renewal. The writers of *Clergy Renewal* shed light on this confusion:

144

In their beginnings, many universities were connected to the church and religious orders, and a sabbatical was considered a time to experiment, learn anew, or pray and meditate. That understanding, unfortunately, has changed and the academic sabbatical has come to be seen as a time for achievement. With the growth of academia's "publish or perish" syndrome, some have lost the view of sabbatical as a time for rest, renewal, and hope.

It is not hard to see how this lack of shared understanding might create conflicting expectations all the way around, causing leaders to miss out on the gift of sabbatical as God offers it to us. Somewhere along the way we replaced God's original idea of sabbatical and its underlying assumptions with a very different thing altogether. I wonder if we would do ourselves a favor by distinguishing these very different experiences and calling the academic model a "study leave" so we can maintain use of the word *sabbatical* in a way that is more tightly connected to the biblical meaning of the root word *shabbat*.

Fortunately for me, our board was very clear about the purpose and intent for my sabbatical. There was no confusion among us, and this gave me a healthy sense of accountability for making decisions that were consistent with the purposes we had clarified together.

The Transforming Center understands sabbatical to be a time of physical and spiritual renewal, which encompasses rest, spiritual direction, and other activities that are restorative and life-giving. We understand sabbatical in the Biblical context, rather than an academic context, and offer sabbatical leave so individuals can recover their

145

vital energies while being disengaged from the everyday demands of ministry. We anticipate that those who take sabbatical return to their work with renewed energy, spiritual vision, and effectiveness. Given that the CEO of the Transforming Center plans and leads worship, preaches, provides pastoral care and overall direction for the organization, we feel it appropriate to cover any and all expenses for restorative activities as approved by the board.

This statement of shared understanding that the sole purpose of sabbatical was rest, rejuvenation, and soul care was approved instantly and unanimously by our board and it has now become an important part of our DNA.

In a sabbath community, sabbatical is a gift from the good people serving on our boards, vestries, and sessions, and the congregations they represent, but let's be clear that these folks are really mediators and facilitators of a gift that comes from God. Knowing that sabbatical is a gift *from a loving God*—and not merely a gift from one's church or institution—makes quite a difference; or at least it did for me. Rather than feeling guilty or entitled, I was able to gratefully receive sabbatical as God's *care* for me, a beloved child. When I doubted whether I deserved such a thing, whether we could afford such a thing, whether this was another facet of privilege, I heard God say, *You've done enough. It's time for you to rest now. I've got this.*

This commitment to unplug completely from work and achievement did mean that I had to work very intentionally to prepare our organization for this sabbatical season—writing articles and other communications that would go out while I was away, recording a podcast season that would air while I was gone, meeting with all my direct reports and trying to provide whatever they might need to flourish in their work while I was away. I am not necessarily proud of how hard I had to work in order to be able to really unplug; I wish it were easier for a key leader in any environment to break away. But ours is a small organization, and at some point I just had to accept that getting away for an extended period of time *is* challenging for leaders and their churches or organizations. What buoyed me was knowing that my coworkers would have what they needed and that we had prepared well for my absence; this was a concrete way of loving them as they were loving me so well by granting this much-needed gift. And it contributed to the sense of peace all of us needed to navigate this new terrain.

FACING OUR CONTRADICTIONS

Away, but with the rpm of my soul still revving, I realized I needed guidance to help me settle down and enter into this strange but blessed season. I was surprised to discover that there were very few resources to support and guide these longer seasons of rest and renewal. The first book I took down from my shelf was *Sabbatical Journey* by Henri Nouwen and, much to my chagrin, even this spiritual master filled his year-long sabbatical with publishing projects and meetings with editors, travel and speaking, officiating at weddings and funerals, social engagements and dinner parties, which both enlivened and drained him. Perhaps his sabbatical had been set up in this way, but one of the constant themes in his sabbatical journal was his attempt to understand the depth of his fatigue and his inner conflict about actually receiving the gift of rest and renewal.

In a journal entry on September 11, 1995, he writes,

Why am I so tired? Although I have all the time I want to sleep, I wake up with an immense feeling of fatigue and get up only because I want to do some work. But I feel extremely frustrated. I want to write, read, and respond to some people's requests, but everything requires an immense effort, and after a few hours of work I collapse in utter exhaustion, often falling into a deep sleep. I expected I would be tired after the intense and busy summer, but now, after ten quiet days, it feels that the more I rest the more tired I become. There seems no end to it.

In that same entry Nouwen acknowledges his own contradictions, letting the reader in on a conversation with a friend that (how can I say this nicely?) nailed him. He admits,

I am quite possessive about my time. I want to use it well and realize some of my long-cherished plans. I can't tolerate wasting time, even though I was to write about wasting time with God, with friends, or with the poor! There are so many contradictions within me. Hans keeps laughing at me. "You are here to relax, to turn off your busyness, but you are living your vacation as a big job!" He is right, but the distance between insight and practice is huge.

Indeed, the distance between insight and practice *is* huge for most of us who are active in Christian work and ministry—or really any work at all. Although we know God built sabbath rhythms of work, rest, and renewal into the world God created—modeling it by ceasing work on the seventh day, instructing humans to rest from their labors on the seventh day, giving periodic rest to laboring animals, letting farmland go fallow every seventh year—there is always the temptation to live as though we can do without them.

148

Nouwen is not alone in his struggle to make peace with his desperate need for rest and his drivenness toward being productive, and his honesty about this made his book a welcome companion during my own sabbatical. It fostered a sense of intimacy with the man himself, offering wonderful questions and spiritual insights to reflect on, and further grounding me in the wonderful opportunity a sabbatical can be, even in the midst of feeling conflicted. His very struggle was endearing and normalized my own and yet I kept wondering if he knew what a sabbatical really *was,* given how hard he worked during that time, how distracted he was by relationships he invested in, and how much he traveled while longing to be settled. His experience was far from what I understood my own sabbatical to be about, and sadly, three weeks after he returned from his sabbatical, he died from a massive heart attack. This gave the reading of his final work an even greater sense of gravitas—as in, this is really serious stuff! No doubt at least part of the exhaustion that was such a constant theme in his journal was attributable to the fact that his heart wasn't working well, and one wishes he could have discovered this while there might have been time to do something about it.

Sobered by all of this and given my own temptations toward constant work and productivity, I knew I needed guidance for traversing this strange and untrodden path. I discovered that even many experienced spiritual directors have never had a sabbatical themselves and so have little experience from which to draw to guide others in this important practice. This gave me pause but in the end, it was a blessing I did not find a one-stop shop that offered all the guidance I was looking for. Instead, I was forced to "go deep"—within myself, with God, and within our Judeo-Christian tradition—to discover the guidance I needed.

CLAIMING SABBATICAL AS GOD'S GIFT TOO

Given the importance of distinguishing between the biblical concept of sabbatical and the development of the academic sabbatical, some churches and denominations have set aside the term *sabbatical* in favor of words like "renewal leave" (versus "study leave"), or have added adjectives like "ecclesiastical" or "ministry" to *sabbatical*. While I am glad for these attempts at clarity, I do find myself wanting to drive a stake in the ground around the use of the word *sabbatical*—to reclaim it if you will—because it is such a richly biblical word grounded in God's knowledge of us, God's desire for us, and the rhythms God built into the world God made. The concept of sabbatical, in particular, emerges from what we observe in nature and in the rhythms of agricultural life mentioned earlier (Exodus 23:10-11).

What a relief it was to realize that sabbatical is, in some ways, as simple as applying all we know and have experienced with sabbath-keeping to a longer and more intentional period of time set apart for rest, renewal, and delight. In fact, just as sabbath is the first thing set apart by God as holy in the Old Testament, sabbatical should also be seen as holy—that is, time set apart for the same holy purpose of allowing the soil of our souls to lie fallow and to experience the new life that dormancy eventually produces. This understanding showed me the way to sabbatical as an opportunity to give myself even more fully to the truths, the principles, and the dynamics of sabbath-keeping as I had already been experiencing them, only now letting them expand and deepen. Knowing the true meaning of sabbatical and Who it comes from made it possible to give myself over to one more facet of the God-ordained rhythms God has built into the universe. We just can't let go of a word that says all that!

150

Turns out that the best preparation for sabbatical, then, is to have engaged in a regular, disciplined practice of sabbath-keeping so that you understand the inner dynamics of it. What is most helpful in our quest for sabbatical time is to fully grasp it as *a spiritual concept rooted in all we know and believe about the sabbath*—indeed, to understand it as a natural progression from sabbath one day a week to experiencing sabbath as a way of life. Sabbatical then becomes simply another facet of sabbath living, a next step in learning to give ourselves *to God* beyond all the work we do *for God,* believing that God can keep running the world while we step away. These longer periods of letting go of human striving while trusting ourselves to God confronts our ego, our grandiosity, and our compulsion in ways that shorter periods of time away simply do not. It creates space for a *season* of self-care and soul care that is beyond what can take place during one day a week.

A COMMUNAL OFFERING

One of the reasons I was hesitant for quite some time about sabbatical is that I am close to people who work in secular vocations and do not get sabbaticals—people like my own husband, who is a banker. In fact, I know this can be a point of resistance on elder boards when the topic of a sabbatical for the pastor is raised. (Fortunately, this is beginning to change as corporate America is now seeing the benefit of giving executive leaders extended time away for a change of pace, new experiences that help them think new thoughts, an opportunity to assess where they are in their career, etc.)

In response to this line of questioning, it is important to call attention to the unique stresses of pastoral and ministry leadership. In addition to being "the buck stops here" person, pastors and senior leaders of ministry organizations are often "on call" at all hours of the day and night to respond to pastoral care needs, and their weekends are taken up with preaching and other church activities to the extent that they rarely get two days off in a row. Especially for solo pastors or leaders of non-profit ministries that are chronically understaffed, there comes a time when sabbath-keeping is not enough to deal with the levels of exhaustion that accumulate over time within schedules that have far less boundaries than the typical nine-to-five job.

As one pastor put it,

> The treadmill metaphor was very real for me in my own ministry, because there was little relief from the pressure of the Sunday morning deadline, virtually no let-up in the seven-day schedule of meetings, study, counseling, and visitation, community, and denominational commitments and little sense of making headway. I would complete one service and sermon only to be confronted with the challenge of another, seven days hence.

When this has been our pattern for a long time, more is required in order to fully attend to aspects of our self that have perhaps been put off or ignored as we have continually poured ourselves out for others. Similarly, high-level lay leaders (like elders and deacons) who work demanding jobs during the week and then show up on evenings and weekends to volunteer at church simply do not have the same boundaries and limits as those who do not take on these responsibilities. They should be given consideration as well when it comes to thinking about sabbatical.

While I am glad the value of sabbatical is beginning to be acknowledged in secular settings, it is important to claim the biblical nature of sabbatical as a deeply spiritual concept that requires trust in the God who made us and who is still at work holding things together and moving things along even when we are resting. In fact, it takes a certain trust in the One who's "got the whole world in his hands" to let go in the way sabbatical requires; it is part of how we build trust into the very fabric of our beings. It is a God-ordained pattern that we work six years and experience at least some dormancy in the seventh—whether we need it or not!

"Churches grow and thrive under long-term pastorates," pastor David Alves points out in his book *A Sabbatical Primer*, and sabbatical goes a long way in ensuring a pastor's ability to stay and minister within a long-term commitment to one congregation. If the congregation or organization is able to give the time as well as the funds for the sabbatical, it removes another stressor and makes it more possible to envision what this time needs to be. Funds for travel, retreat expenses, spiritual direction, psychological counseling, a class, a nutritionist and/ or trainer to give concerted attention to physical well-being— all of these cost money; if funds are provided, a leader is more apt to build what they need into their sabbatical experience and come back stronger and healthier. Whatever the sabbatical costs, it is a small price to pay to ensure the long-term commitment *and* the long-term health and well-being of one of your ministry's greatest assets.

What Your Soul Wants to Say to God

As with all spiritual practices, we begin with desire that deepens into intentionality and is eventually lived out through a plan, which is the subject of chapter eleven. Sabbatical in particular is such a radical discipline—to let go of the plow for anywhere from three to six months or even a year—that we need to be in touch with our longing, we need to wrestle through our resonance and our resistance, and maybe even fight with our sense of impossibility of it all. Do not shrink back from the emotions you are feeling right now—the desire and the experience of feeling drawn, but also wondering if sabbatical is even possible.

Pull out your journal or a notebook and talk to God about this. Express to God directly all you are feeling and experiencing as you consider God's provision of sabbatical. If you have a hard time getting started, begin with the phrase "God, what I most want to say to you now is . . ." and then just let it rip! You do not need to share this with anyone, so be as honest as you can be. For now, let it be enough to pour out your desire and your need to God. Please take some time with this—maybe even a few days or weeks—because this will become the foundation of your sabbatical planning.

If you are a leader in a church community or a ministry organization, consider setting aside some time in your meeting schedule to reflect on establishing a pattern of sabbatical leave for pastors or senior leaders as part of your commitment to sabbath-keeping in community. Assign someone who has passion around this to lead the conversation about the ways in which God built this pattern into our world and what you believe about it now. Do you have anything like this already built into your life together? If so, describe what you already have in place in clear terms and revisit it—assess how you are doing with living out this value, reaffirm your commitment to it, and maybe even further develop it.

Don't wait for your pastor and other significant leaders to burn out and then have to come to you to ask for a sabbatical as a way of averting crisis. Instead, get out ahead of it; determine which leadership roles should be eligible for sabbatical and at what intervals. Everyone wins when clergy are granted periodic chunks of renewal leave. Pastors remain vital and healthy while congregations receive the benefits of engaged, long-term pastorates, new lay ministry skills, and exciting opportunities for mission . . . this is a very progressive way lay leaders can ensure the best of clergy leadership over the long haul.

11

MORE THAN
a VACATION

● ● ●

A sabbatical is not a vacation. It is a different kind of work—
it is a directed time of refreshment and restoration. It is a
time for drawing closer and listening more carefully, with
the intent of deeper intimacy with God. It can involve
reading, writing, and wrestling in prayer—especially
wrestling with the tendency to be busy, wrestling to let
go, to jump off the performance-go-round, and relax.

DAVID ALVES

A SABBATICAL MAY START with a vacation, end with a vacation, or include a vacation, but it is not in itself a vacation. A vacation, by definition, is usually a shorter period of time that often includes plans for fun and time spent with the people we love, sightseeing, travel, and lots of activity. Maybe some rest, yes, but many will admit that when they get home they need to rest from their vacation!

If planned well, a sabbatical is different from that. It is a season of *a different kind of intentionality* toward rest and very personal needs, hopes, and desires that will be addressed specifically and concretely in one's sabbatical plan. A sabbatical plan will be unique to each of us—tailored toward what is restful and replenishing for our personality type, the needs we are aware of, desires we are in touch with, what has been going on in our lives leading up to the sabbatical, and God's invitations to us in the midst of it all. While a sabbatical will be consistent with sabbath-keeping in terms of freedom *from* drivenness and over-identification with productivity, all while fostering freedom *for* rest, replenishment, worship, and delight, the specifics will vary tremendously.

For instance, my sabbatical was preceded by a great deal of loss—personal loss and losses in my ministry life. I needed a vacation (or two or three) but I also needed more than a vacation; I needed healing. I needed time, space, and support for grieving and bringing good closure to the season of living near my parents and caring for them, and I needed to orient myself to the new season I was entering into. In addition I was longing for a break from the heartache of the past ministry season; I needed distance from the hard decisions I had been forced to make, restoration of what it took out of me each time I had to communicate about those decisions, and rest from carrying not just my own grief but others' grief as well.

Beyond the specifics of that particular season, I needed a complete break from life in ministry and the exhaustion that accumulates over time, even with a regular sabbath practice in place. I was, quite simply, done; I could not go any further.

PLANNING FOR SABBATICAL

The Alban Institute, which produces and distributes research-based information on how to minister more effectively, recommends that the timing of one's sabbatical be written into the terms of one's call or into the contract to serve in a ministry organization. They go so far as to say that "jointly committing to sabbatical leave from the beginning of one's service in a congregation or agency is crucial to the eventual success of the sabbatical itself." This is solid wisdom and counsel! Hopefully the church, denomination, or ministry organization already has a sabbatical policy in place and the call or employment documents acknowledge this policy so everyone involved understands and affirms this commitment. This means that technically the planning for sabbatical starts right from the get-go and all long-range ministry and financial planning will take this into account.

With that long-term perspective in place, it is customary for leaders and their boards to take six to twelve months (or even longer) to start making more specific and detailed plans about how much travel will be involved, what it will take to cover the pastor's or leader's responsibilities, a plan for funding the sabbatical, and so forth. And that doesn't include the time it may take to get in touch with our deepest needs and desires for this time. Most leaders have been moving so fast for so long that that we may be quite out of touch with our souls—what we need, what we long for, and God's invitations to us.

Dr. Frank Nieman observed that Roman Catholic clergy who take part in three-to-nine-month sabbatical programs often have difficulty pinpointing what they need in a sabbatical: "What they say they want isn't what they need, and what helps

159

one doesn't help another." That's why most of us need a spiritual director or someone experienced in sabbatical guidance to listen along with us as we attend deeply to ourselves and to God. Then, based on this shared listening, they can help us formulate a plan that corresponds to what we are hearing and even walk with us during this significant time when a lot will happen, spiritually speaking.

It will also take time and careful planning to educate or remind our congregation about the value of sabbatical as part of the community's commitment to sabbath living, and to communicate about the particulars of the sabbatical as they become clear. Also it will take time and careful thought to plan not only for how the needs of the congregation or ministry are going to be cared for, but to cast vision and plan for how the congregation will actually benefit and receive gifts while we are away.

While the idea of planning might sound a bit cerebral, in my experience the planning phase can actually be quite tender and soulful because it forces us to get in touch with our needs and longings in order to be really honest with God and others as we plan. We might also experience some fear and anxiety about whether sabbatical will actually work (will I really be able to let go?), whether our ministry or congregation will be able to get along without us, or even worse, if they will do just fine! I remember one pastor sharing with me during his sabbatical that he was quite unnerved that his congregation was doing so well without him and that his young colleague was doing just fine handling funerals and other pastoral care ministries while he was away. Fortunately this pastor was mature enough to laugh at himself, recognizing this as God's challenge to his sense of indispensability and a means of humbling him in a good way.

The planning phase is also a time of high hopes—knowing what we want and need our sabbatical to be, striving to hold out until we get there, wondering if it can possibly meet our expectations and accomplish all we need it to accomplish. I remember a feeling of unreality about it all as well—like I wasn't sure it was really going to happen, like it sounded too good to be true. And yet I found that writing a thoughtful plan that was grounded in the realities of my life (including a global pandemic!) was very beneficial and made it more real. Planning not only helped me structure this gift of time with greater intentionality but it also provided something I could reference *during* sabbatical to keep me grounded in my intent and able to make good choices consistent with that intent.

ESTABLISHING GOALS

My plan was simpler than some I have seen, partly because of the limits imposed by the Covid-19 pandemic (retreat centers were closed, travel was risky and ill-advised, and there were few in-person classes or learning opportunities to take advantage of), and partly because I was not applying for a major grant, so I didn't have to convince anyone of anything; since my organization was making funds available for this, I was relieved of the burden and pressure of trying to "make a case." God used even the limits of the pandemic to "hem me in" (as the psalmist writes about in Psalm 139) and help me stay focused on what was most needed rather than being overwhelmed by unlimited options.

My goals for this time were simple: rest, replenishment, delight, listening to God in the depths of my own soul. They were not lofty, in any sense, but they were my words that came

161

straight out of my own need and desire. I was longing to enjoy God for my own soul's sake after years of pouring out and guiding others in their enjoyment of God. I was longing to pull back from ministry and organizational leadership, which by definition requires an outward focus—a focus on being present to God on others' behalf, being what others need me to be, and listening for what they need me to listen for. I longed to listen to God for myself in utter privacy and to be more rested when I was with God—which seemed like the greatest gift I could imagine. And the beauty of it all is that I didn't need to go anywhere for that! I found my familiarity with the dynamics of sabbath-keeping to be really helpful; in fact, I'm not sure I would have articulated these goals so naturally and easily—or even felt they were worthy enough—if I had not been so steeped in sabbath-keeping.

HOPES AND DREAMS

After establishing these basic goals, I created space to begin articulating my hopes and dreams for this time. I had seen other sabbatical proposals that included language like "program rationale and design," but that kind of language was rather deadening. It put me in the frame of mind—not soul—of needing to prove something to others, or convince someone of something, and maybe even prove something to myself. I was grateful I did not have to do any of that because what was drawing me into sabbatical was so intimate, tender, and per-sonal that to have to prove anything (including the value of sabbatical itself) to myself or anyone else would have kept me in the performance mindset so common to those who are in leadership. My sabbatical plan needed to come not from my

162

mind but from listening to my soul. So I wrote about my hopes and dreams, and framing it this way caused the plan to flow quite effortlessly in the following categories. I offer them here because they may be helpful to others' planning.

Get deep rest and replenishment—for body, mind, and soul. We need to take time to reflect on what constitutes rest for us on all three of these levels. We should not underestimate the significance of real rest and how long it will take for us to unplug fully—enough to start sleeping well (rest for the body), to stop thinking about work and let go of concerns we might still be holding (rest for the mind), and to let go of our persona and any façade we maintain (rest for the soul)—in order to be a child in God's presence, just being with God with what is. There is no microwaving this part of the process and it happens gradually, so we must give plenty of time and space in our plan.

David Alves, in his book *A Sabbatical Primer for Pastors*, wisely points out that

Sabbatical is an intentional release from stressors and overwhelming spiritual and people demands. It is a re-charging of the battery. Serotonin is a neurotransmitter essential not only to your survival, but to your sense of well-being and vascular health. Prolonged stress depletes serotonin levels. Once a person's levels are depleted, those levels are not restored by a good night's sleep . . . it's more like a trickle-charge needed to replenish sero-tonin to healthy levels. . . . Any less than three months is truly not enough time for the physical/health benefits of a sabbatical—the restoration of Serotonin/5-hydroxy-tryptamine (5-HT) levels and the readjustment of the body to less adrenaline. Low serotonin levels are associated with mood disorders, particularly depression. Many pastors and ministry leaders operate in "fight or flight" mode most of their days and nights. That's how they appear tireless. But this constant motion depletes their 5-HT levels . . . and these levels must be restored for the body to function as it was originally designed to function.

This is why I recommend four to six months for sabbatical if possible—so we can spend at least the first month learning how to sleep and rest again, allowing serotonin levels to return to healthy levels and receiving the healing that happens during long, deep, regular sleep. We cannot—and I repeat, cannot—underestimate how much resting we will need. Since sabbatical time is in addition to normal vacation, we can consider starting our sabbatical with a week or two of vacation to get a head start on resting. If resting was all we did on sabbatical, that would be enough!

Find delight. As I let myself dream about what sabbatical time might be like, I recognized a deep desire for time and space to simply delight in God's good and most basic gifts—life in my body, my home (which I love), and my loved ones: my husband, children, grandchildren, and friends. It was a tender awareness when I acknowledged that caring for my parents (which was its own gift and privilege) coupled with the intensity of the preceding ministry season had robbed me of time and space to be fully available to these gifts. I wanted to reclaim and reconnect with the gifts of my life by simply having more time to be present and enjoy them rather than shoehorning them into such a demanding schedule. And I wanted

164

to chart out a new way forward that would allow me to be present with these gifts long term. Because I travel quite a bit for my work, it was clear that staying put and enjoying the gifts of home would be good for my soul. I wanted to stop pushing and just receive.

One of the things that was simply amazing to me is that, once I had fully let go of work responsibilities, I experienced so much simple joy in putzing (is that really a word?) around my house and yard, doing small projects I hadn't had time for in years, reading, going on walks and bike rides, cooking and trying new recipes, working out several times a week, being more available to engage with my children and grandchildren, and sleeping long and well in my own bed. I was happy *every day* and realized I did not have to go anywhere or do anything grand in order to feel simply delighted with my life, allowing God's rest to seep into me. I discovered that rest cannot be forced; it can only be received. This experience of taking simple pleasure in life's ordinary gifts reminds me of a passage from Katherine May's book *Wintering:*

> I have always been a cook. But in the last few years, cooking has been pushed out of my life, along with its accompanying pleasure of shopping for ingredients. Life has been busy, and in the general rush of things, these vital fragments of my identity have been squeezed out. I have missed them, but in a shrugging kind of way. What can you do when you're already doing everything? The problem with "everything" is that it ends up looking an awful lot like nothing: just one long haze of frantic activity, with all the meaning sheared away.

One phrase that stands out is "these vital fragments of my identity." The things we love, enjoy, and delight in are not merely incidental, they are not meaningless luxuries we indulge in on sabbatical. They are vital fragments of our identity that often get lost in the rush of our busy lives. Sabbatical gives us the chance to reconnect with these vital elements of ourselves, which is why they are disproportionately energizing—it is because we are reconnecting with pieces of ourselves as we have been created by God, and there is no better, cleaner energy than just being the person God created us to be.

So, what are the delightful gifts God has given to each of us that we have not been able to fully receive and enjoy as of late? What are the things we love and delight in just because God made us that way—with gifts, interests, and passions? And how can we craft our sabbatical to include more of these?

For one pastor I know, brewing beer is not only a love and a passion but also a contemplative practice. He says,

> After I graduated from seminary, a friend gave me a book entitled *Brew Like a Monk,* and the vision of this book—the combined focus on the practices of both brewing beer and living the monastic life—has made my heart sing ever since. Brewing like a monk is a contemplative way of seeing God in every aspect of life. The process helps me cultivate gratitude for the gift of life as I work. I have fallen deeply in love with the process of brewing—mashing grain, boiling hops, pitching the yeast to do its fermentation magic, and finally, after waiting for 3–4 weeks, tasting the beer. Similarly, I have also found great joy in

immersing myself in the pace, rhythm, and practices of monastic communities.

Given this delight, his sabbatical plan included several retreats, taking a course on beer quality and analysis, apprenticing at a brewery, learning how to build brewing equipment and studying the science of brewing, and then actually brewing beer.

Another pastor identified biking as "a place of sanctuary," longing for the open roads to have time to reflect, think, and pray. And because he is energized by challenging himself physically, his sabbatical plan was to bike across America—a lifelong dream that would not have been possible for him before he experienced a process of transformation in which he dropped seventy-two pounds, adopted a healthier lifestyle and began competing in various athletic events, including the Ironman. His physical transformation was an outward sign of his inner transformation, which resulted in a greater emphasis on physical health and wellness along with an emphasis on spiritual practices, and he wanted to lean into these gifts even further. His congregation was thrilled to offer him a three-month sabbatical that began with a three-day spiritual retreat to invite God into his sabbatical. Then he drove to California to begin his trek across the nation to the East Coast—biking approximately one hundred miles a day and dipping his tires in the ocean on both coasts—with his wife following along in an RV so they could sleep in "their own bed" along the way.

Travel or stay home. Travel is commonly considered one of the key ingredients for an effective sabbatical because it disconnects us from our place of living and working, disrupting our normal patterns so that we are open to new and fresh perspectives. But that doesn't mean we have to travel to far-off lands. It just means that we want to build in enough "getting away" that such disconnection and disruption can occur. We can pay attention to a place or places where we have simply been happy; it doesn't even have to be that far away, it just needs to make us feel as though we are away and that it ushers us into a happy and unencumbered way of being.

For years my happy place has been the shores of Lake Michigan. It's the next best thing to an ocean (no sharks) and it is within driving distance, so I can pack anything and everything I want to have with me into my own car (including a laundry basket full of books, an egg poacher, my personal blender for morning smoothies) and drive. Because I fly a lot for work, packing all my things in the car and the drive itself are a blessing, allowing me to gradually let go rather than face the stress of airports and air travel. So I started my sabbatical with a driving trip to give myself a hard stop and to aid the process of letting go and entering into deep rest. There would be a longer period of time away later, but since I was longing to be at home in my own life, a shorter time away to begin was just right.

For others, getting away and staying away for longer periods might be just the thing—especially if we can stay long enough to settle in and rest rather than moving on to new places every other day. The point here is to know ourselves; know what we really need (not just what seems exotic) and plan accordingly.

For many, significant travel to far-off places, historic sites (Christian or otherwise), or even a pilgrimage designed for significant experience and learning will be very life giving and important. Perhaps there is a biblical character or a saint we've always wanted to study or whose footsteps we've wanted to walk in, a religious community we want to immerse in, or a place in the world (like the Holy Land) that we want to experience. Sabbatical is a wonderful opportunity for this kind of travel as long as we don't wear ourselves out and keep ourselves so stimulated and distracted that we miss what's really needed for soul care.

At the very least, consider at least one extended retreat at a retreat center, hopefully with spiritual direction. Many leaders start and end their sabbatical time with a retreat—the first as a way of settling in spiritually, letting go and inviting God into this special time, and the second to create space for capturing what God has spoken to us during sabbatical time and to prepare for reentry.

Pay attention to personality. One of the things that came clear to me in my planning had to do with my personality type. Myers-Briggs is a helpful model for understanding our personality preferences and also what is needed for wholeness. Robert Mulholland discusses the Myers-Briggs typology and how understanding it contributes to our spiritual formation. In his book *Invitation to a Journey,* he encourages us to use this knowledge of ourselves to provide our natural personality with what it needs and also to stretch ourselves toward developing personality traits that are underdeveloped. I am a *P* (*perceiving*) on the Myers-Briggs typology, which means I prefer to experience the world through spontaneity rather than structure, leaving things open-ended rather than buttoning things up, using a laid-back approach rather than being too tied down, letting things unfold rather than being bound by a detailed and restrictive schedule. My life on the other hand requires a lot of everything I am not—structure, plans, schedules, and agendas— and while necessary, this is a source of exhaustion.

As I approached my sabbatical, I realized I was exhausted at the level of personality and was longing to lean into my personality preferences a bit more—freedom to be spontaneous, to pick up and take short trips/day trips, to let days unfold. And I knew that giving myself a lot of this during sabbatical would be an important aspect of replenishment for this Myers-Briggs *P* who, of necessity, has to live such a scheduled life! This turned out to be one of the best things about my sabbatical.

As we prepare for sabbatical it might be an interesting exercise to refresh our awareness of our personality type, notice the personality preferences we don't get to experience as much as we would like, and make sure our sabbatical time is structured more for what we prefer and naturally enjoy! For a *J* (*judging*) personality, having days, weeks, and months fairly scheduled out and then following the schedule might bring great joy. For the *T* (*thinker*), it might mean the world to take a class or develop a reading list that will challenge and expand intellect. For an *I* (*introvert*), to settle into a rhythm of days that includes the luxury of more time alone and "going deep" with a few people rather than large group activity will be just the thing. For the *E* (*extrovert*), accessing groups and gatherings regularly during this time, but not the usual community we work with and minister to, is vital. Sabbatical is a time to nourish and replenish the personality God gave us, while perhaps also building in a couple things that will stretch us toward other preferences that require energy to engage fully.

Care for and strengthen our body. As I planned for my sabbatical, I realized the previous several years had really taken a toll on my physical self. I hadn't been sleeping well for a long time due to the care and concern I was holding. There had been little time for walking (a love of mine) or working out because I was juggling so much in my work life due to our organizational downsizing. Plus, I was stopping to visit and care for my parents on the way home most nights. It was routine for me to work long days, stop by to see my parents, and then get home late—completely exhausted, hungry, and not able to do anything but collapse and eat unhealthy food. In addition, I was attending my parents' medical appointments and procedures while putting off my own. I knew better than to neglect my body in these ways, and after my parents had completed their journeys in their bodies, I longed to have time and space to care for and strengthen my own body again.

A significant part of my sabbatical planning was to schedule doctors' appointments and medical procedures, as well as line up a personal trainer who could assess where I was, develop a plan, coach, and train me throughout this time. It was such a blessing to start becoming healthy again in my body and to feel myself getting stronger! Harking back to the sobering reality of Henri Nouwen's untimely and unexpected heart attack, I encourage everyone to schedule a physical and doctors' appointments related to medical concerns before sabbatical or early on in sabbatical so there is spacious time to deal with new discoveries that need to be addressed.

Another small but important part of my sabbatical time was observing how wonderful it was to go to doctors' appointments not stressed about work that wasn't getting done or people I was inconveniencing, not stressed if an appointment started or ran late, and relaxed enough to sit and read a magazine rather than making phone calls and answering email in the waiting room. I know, I know, it's ridiculous that this is even a thing, but for me it really was, and it felt delicious. So as we prepare for sabbatical, we build in time to pay attention to and then care for our bodies. In our care for others, both at home and at work, we may have neglected caring for the temple of our bodies; sabbatical is a natural space to correct this imbalance.

What Your Soul Wants to Say to God

We're not finished with all that can be considered in sabbatical planning quite yet, but let's stop here and take time to reflect on the categories described in the chapter. Perhaps you can step away for several hours or even a day of retreat time to sink and settle into your own body and soul and listen in that place where God's spirit witnesses with your spirit about things that are true. Or take your morning solitude to feel your longing and to reflect on what would mean the most to you during a sabbatical season. Let the words and examples offered in this chapter prime the pump for articulating what you need and want, and let your thoughts and ideas flow in response to the following questions/categories:

What am I hearing from God regarding God's invitation to sabbatical time?

What would I like to see happen during this sabbatical time?

What are my hopes and dreams?

If you have trouble getting started, pull out your journal or a legal pad and write across the top: What I am hoping for and dreaming of for my sabbatical is . . . and then just write. Don't censor yourself or hold back at all. No one else has to see what you are writing here because you will still create a more formal plan for others to see when you are ready.

- *What are my hopes and dreams for rest and replenishment?*

- *What would bring me delight? What gifts from God do I want to delight in?*

- *How does travel fit into my needs and desires?*

- *What does my personality need to experience in order to find refreshment and replenishment?*

- *What does my body need and what would I like to experience in my body? What will I need to do to arrange for that?*

It might take several times of quiet to fully articulate what you are needing in these areas, so take as much time as you need. In chapter twelve we reflect more deeply on the spiritual opportunities contained within sabbatical.

12

A SEASON *of* SPIRITUAL OPPORTUNITY

● ● ○

Free at last! Free to think critically, to feel deeply,
and to pray as never before. Free to write about the many
experiences that I have stored up in my heart and mind
during the last nine years. Free to deepen friendships
and explore new ways of loving. Free most of all to fight
with the Angel of God and ask for a new blessing.

HENRI NOUWEN

WHATEVER ELSE SABBATICAL IS, it is most surely a time of spiritual possibility that is quite different from other kinds of time away. The quote above, from the very first page of Henri Nouwen's sabbatical journal, expresses the strong sense of spiritual possibility he experienced as he approached this set-apart time. Just before that he writes,

I feel strange! Very happy and very scared at the same time. I have always dreamt of a whole year without appointments, meetings, lectures, travels, letters, and phone calls, a year completely open to let something radical happen. But can I do it? Can I let go of all the things that make me feel useful and significant? I realize I am quite addicted to being busy and experience a bit of withdrawal anxiety. I have to nail myself to my chair and control these wild impulses to get up again and becoming busy with whatever draws my attention.

Nouwen is expressing what I call the "push-pull phenomenon"— an inner experience that often indicates an invitation from God is real precisely because we feel drawn and yet have some level of resistance or discomfort all at the same time. Noticing this phenomenon can help us recognize that God is at work opening up spiritual opportunities. The expansiveness of sabbatical time—and the fact that trying to work and be productive in our normal ways is prohibited—means that other kinds of desires and intentions have the opportunity to flourish at the forefront of our hearts and minds rather than being tamped down. So, what are some of the spiritual opportunities embedded in sabbatical time, and how can we plan for them?

DEEPENING YOUR SPIRITUAL PRACTICES

One aspect of sabbatical I looked forward to and longed for the most was time and space to deepen spiritual practices I was already familiar with, along with exploring others that were fresh and new. Although I have taught, written, and shared about spiritual practices in many different ways, sabbatical was a welcome opportunity to experience spiritual practices as new channels for the living water of God's refreshing presence to find its way into the scorched, empty places of my heart and soul. The longing to open up to God in new and more intentional ways was fierce; I wonder if you feel it, too.

I felt most drawn to deepen my practice of Centering Prayer. I was already very committed to Centering Prayer, but I felt sabbatical would offer the opportunity to be even more disciplined in ordering my life for it by incorporating two prayer periods a day rather than just one. I pulled *The Daily Reader for Contemplative Living,* a compilation of excerpts from the writings of Fr. Thomas Keating, off my shelf for daily support. I also took a course on Centering Prayer that included seven full-day offerings of in-depth spiritual study on the conceptual background that supports a faithful practice, a heightened awareness of the purification process that takes place through the practice of Centering Prayer, and help discerning when psychological skills can be helpful tools. Perfect!

There are other practices we may know and have practiced but now we feel drawn to deepen, such as lectio divina (maybe with a group), a journaling workshop, welcoming prayer, guided meditation with pottery or art, iconography, yoga and other kinds of body work, fly fishing, walking meditation, or even a spirituality of golf! What distinguishes spiritual practice from mere skill building or entertainment is that we engage the activity with the clear intention of creating new avenues for connecting with God, and we support that intent with guidance from others who have wisdom and experience to offer.

ATTENDING TO OUR INNER LIFE

I am a firm believer in spiritual direction *and* therapy as part of one's sabbatical plan. Hopefully we already have these resources in place when we need them, but if not, try to put them in place before sabbatical season. And if possible, see if the expenses associated with this can be included in your sabbatical funding. In Christian ministry we are on the front lines of a spiritual battle all the time, and in any real battle there are wounds that need healing, victories that need celebrating, learnings that need to be captured, and new approaches to consider. While we might bring the same issues to both spiritual direction and therapy, how they are approached in each of these relationships is distinct.

In spiritual direction, the director creates hospitable space for us to be attentive to the presence of God in our life and deep within our soul. They will ask open-ended, Spirit-guided questions such as: Where is God in that for you? What happens when you pray about that? When you are quiet, what do hear God saying? When do you feel most alive these days? When do you experience life draining from you? What might it look like for you to choose more of that which gives you life? What do you really want? Spiritual directors might make suggestions and give support for our spiritual practices (very valuable on sabbatical and any time) but they will rarely, if ever, give advice.

A therapist, on the other hand, is expected to give learned advice—that is, information and guidance regarding what will contribute to our psychological health and wholeness. If we are humans living among others in families and friendships, work and ministry, life is always throwing things at us that hurt, confuse, and confound. We might as well accept the fact that continuing to journey toward psychological health and wholeness, learning to respond in a healthy manner, and identifying unproductive patterns and establishing new ones is an ongoing process that will not be complete until we see Jesus face to face. Sabbatical is the perfect opportunity for a psychological checkup and tune-up because we have time to follow up on anything that needs ongoing attention.

It may sound odd, but one of the greatest and most restorative gifts of my sabbatical was time and space for a different level of engagement in spiritual direction and therapy. I had been noticing that it was hard for either one of these to be as meaningful as it could be in the crush of everyday life. I would enter into these sessions distracted by my work or concerned about being unreachable to my coworkers. Then when the session was over, I would get pulled back into pressing concerns almost immediately and lose my grip on some of the insight and awareness I was coming into. And yet, there were really important things stirring in my soul and happening in my life that needed more focused spiritual and psychological attention.

Identifying this frustration caused me to plan into my sabbatical a rhythm of spiritual direction and therapy every other week, in which I was able to take time before each session to prepare what I wanted to bring and after each session to reflect and journal in order to further process and capture what God was saying. It was *so* rich and productive to be able to do this.

One of the surprises that emerged from making this a priority was noticing that the death of both of my parents freed me to be more honest about some of the hard dynamics present in my family of origin, to understand its effect on me, and to do the work of finding freedom from the weight and the bondage of it. I realized that my "grief work" was not so much about the loss of my parents as much as it was about recognizing what had been broken in my family and grieving the fact that this would now not be fixed this side of heaven. I needed time and space to acknowledge this, to experience my sadness and work through it, and in the end, to accept it. I shed many tears on my way to deep psychological and spiritual acceptance of some hard realities; I experienced the "good grief" that eventually leads to peace and greater levels of interior rest and freedom. Not having to go right back to work and function immediately following these sessions gave me the opportunity to stay with what got stirred up and do the inner, prayerful work that was needed.

I can just hear what some of you might be thinking—*That doesn't sound very restful at all!* or *That sounds awful, crying all the way through your sabbatical*—but I can say that this aspect of my sabbatical was restful in the deepest sense of the word. It was rest that comes from laying down heavy burdens one has carried for a long time; it was the relief that comes when you've finally looked the most painful realities of your existence square in the face, grieved it all the way to the bottom, and found comfort there rather than using your energy to hold it in or keep it at bay.

Jesus says, "Blessed are those who mourn, for they will be comforted" (Matthew 5:4) and it is true. The rest I was able to enter into, by laying down some heavy burdens I had been carrying for a lifetime, continues to this day. Indeed, I even put important boundaries in place to keep me from picking up those old burdens again and identified some new choices and patterns that will make me a healthier and more rested person for the rest of my days. I emerged from sabbatical different and better for having done this work; I really do not have adequate words to describe the significance this care for my human self was during my sabbatical season. It is a gift that keeps on giving—to myself, my relationships, and my leadership—and, in the end, it was more beneficial than any exotic trip I could have taken.

So whatever you do in your planning, make sure that you are ordering this time around what you most deeply desire and need, not just around superficial wants and distractions. If you do, you can't go wrong and your sabbatical will be what is best for you.

WRITING FOR OUR OWN SOUL'S SAKE

For those who keep a week-in-week-out schedule of preaching, teaching, and pastoral care, there is an inevitable focus on learning things and articulating truth for others that can work against being able to listen to God for our own soul's sake. What this means is that sometimes we find ourselves serving up bread that is only half-baked! If we have been endowed with the gift of eloquence, we might be able to make it sound perfectly done, but the truth is it is pretty doughy on the inside and you wouldn't want anyone to cut too far into it!

One of the occupational hazards of being an up-front communicator and leader is that we may find ourselves writing articles, preaching sermons, and pontificating about our ideas before we should—as in, before we have studied something carefully or experienced something fully. As I approached sabbatical, I recognized a longing to learn things, explore things, read things, and hear things from God that were for myself and not for anyone else—at least not yet. I wanted to let some things incubate and percolate without so much pressure to go public. I wanted to practice hiddenness, where

I could exist for God and God alone in the company of those with whom I am most intimate.

So I actually addressed this in my plan, which invited accountability: *I do not envision writing to publish or taking on a project with a deadline; but since I have been sad for the last several years about not being able to write, it would bring great joy to me to have time, space, and freedom to write whatever bubbles to the surface.* This expression of desire caused me to create a sabbatical journal that would remain private but would provide a record of what had transpired between me and God. I did not write every day like Henri Nouwen did (which became the book *Sabbatical Journey* that others chose to publish after his death), but there were days when I wrote and wrote and wrote. It was an amazing discipline to create this as space for myself and God alone—along the lines of the intimacy of the wilderness described in the book of Hosea: "Therefore, I will now allure her, and bring her into the wilderness, and speak tenderly to her. . . . There she shall respond as in the days of her youth" (Hosea 2:14-15).

I know not everyone likes to journal or even experiences journaling as a helpful spiritual practice, but I would suggest at least procuring a sabbatical journal that can be a place for private communication with God, where you can just see what unfolds. It could also be a journal for art, sketching, or expressing ourselves with color—anything that creates this intimate space for communicating and communing with the Holy One. Sabbatical is a time of great intimacy between ourselves and our Creator; to have a place where we capture what we are experiencing, what we want to say to God, and what God is saying to us can be a very precious thing, even if we haven't journaled before and may never do so again!

LEARNING AND "SHARPENING THE SAW"

Many of us leader types love to learn, whether it is something that has to do with sharpening our vocation skills—taking a class on preaching, church history, worship, leadership, marriage and family counseling, family systems theory as it relates to life in congregations—or learning and practicing something completely unrelated, like bird watching, dance lessons, painting, iconography, creative writing, or fly fishing. While we want to be careful not to fill sabbatical with work and achievement, there is something truly enlivening about learning just for the pleasure of it and getting better at something that relates to your life and work or one of your interests or hobbies. What might that be for you?

I have such a lifelong love of learning, reading, and studying that the idea of having time and space for my own exploration was exciting beyond measure. I participated in one significant learning program and had a wonderful reading list that fully represented all my loves (poetry, novels, biographies) as well as areas of interest that I wanted to become more wise and learned about (race in America, integration of spirituality and psychology, using the Enneagram in spiritual direction). It gave me such pleasure to spend many uninterrupted hours reading without any guilt at all—probably the most time I've had to read since I was an adolescent!

Here again, we need to know ourselves well so that with wisdom and understanding about our own drives and motivations we can honor what is true for us. For some it may feel like a tremendous relief not to do anything that feels academic or achievement oriented, while for others it will feel like a tremendous privilege to take a class for pure interest and pleasure or to read to our heart's content through a care-fully curated reading list!

INVESTING IN FRIENDSHIPS
AND RELATIONSHIPS

People are gifts from God that often get lost in the shuffle of ministry—friends, extended family, colleagues we enjoy and who keep us sharp, and maybe even people from our past we've lost touch with (friends from high school and college, family members who live far away, friends from past work settings, etc.). Sab-batical can be a wonderful time for seeking out those special ones in our lives who enliven us, who matter to us, and whom we simply enjoy. We might consider incorporating visits to friends and extended family into some of our travel or even making them a destination—not so much that we are running around and ex-hausting ourselves but enough that we experience the love and connection God intends for us with the people God has given us.

As I write, our country and our world are still locked down as the Covid-19 virus surges around us, so the idea of traveling and seeing friends feels a bit like fantasy—but I know there will come a day when we can see friends again, not just on zoom but in our living rooms, on our decks, and in fun restaurants. And what a day of rejoicing that will be! Since I had the good fortune of taking my sabbatical in the summer, it was possible to sit with a few friends on decks and patios or simply go for a walk. I also set up spacious times on the phone with friends with whom I am accustomed to listening deeply when we have the chance, and was surprised at the difference being on sabbatical made in the quality of presence I was able to bring when I wasn't so tired and pressed for time.

But again, we can't wear ourselves out. We must pay close attention to our personality type and how much we can do with friends without getting too tired relationally. And we should feel free *not* to schedule relational connections that feel draining or that come from a place of "ought" and "should." Those kinds of relationships are more like work, so we can feel free to save them for after sabbatical.

MAKING SPACE FOR DISCERNMENT

Another unique opportunity on sabbatical is space to ponder the deeper questions of life, to carry with us anything we are needing to discern, holding our lives and vocation open in God's presence to confirm our sense of call or invite us to move in new directions. It might be a time to recognize and mark transitions, noting what questions emerge from this recognition.

One of the questions I carried into my sabbatical time had to do with the future of the Transforming Center and my role in it. There were longings I had been sensing for a long time but found hard to articulate within the constant awareness of knowing what everyone else wanted or needed from me. It was going to take time, space, and freedom from outer and inner distractions to let my life speak in the way I knew it needed to. I knew that when I returned our board would convene and I would need to be prepared to participate in discernment with them, and I knew that my own sense of calling and invitation from God would be a very significant factor in our discernment. I also knew that whatever I had to say upon my return would be received, respected, and honored—which meant that it would have influence—which was wonderful and frightening all at the same time. But how would I carry this into sabbatical without it becoming a weight or a burden or a distraction from resting?

Rather than allowing future conversations and decisions to become weighty or distracting, I disciplined myself early on to just notice whatever I noticed and receive whatever God gave, without fully engaging in trying to discern what I would contribute to those conversations. Up until the last couple weeks. I chose to trust that if I followed God's invitation to rest, what I needed for this discernment would be there when I needed it. On sabbatical, it is not whether we have questions but *how* we hold the questions that really matters. Sabbatical is a time, more than any other, when we can do what Rainer Marie Rilke encourages in his well-loved quote:

> Be patient toward all that is unsolved in your heart and try to love the questions themselves, like locked rooms and like books that are now written in a very foreign tongue. Do not now seek the answers, which cannot be given you because you would not be able to live them. And the point is, to live everything. Live the questions now. Perhaps you will then gradually, without noticing it, live along some distant day into the answer.

If we live the questions in this way throughout our sabbatical time—with great trust in the God who is never early but always right on time—all will be well, and all manner of things will be well. We might call this "resting with our questions" on sabbatical.

Is there a question you are harboring in your heart that you are longing to share with God in a more spacious way than everyday life allows? Let this awareness come, and determine to *rest* with your questions rather than work really hard on your questions, and see what God does with it.

PLANNING FOR REENTRY

Many who have been on a sabbatical report that the most neglected part of their plan was the plan for their reentry, but as David Alves notes,

> Ministry re-entry is one of the most crucial phases of your sabbatical. This is the part . . . you'd be most likely to blow off without some encouragement to the contrary. If you're not careful here, you'll probably lose most of what you've gained within the first few months of your return to ministry.

How do we avoid this pitfall? By including it in our sabbatical planning.

Depending on how long our sabbatical has been, we might plan for anywhere from a week (if it was a three-to-four-month sabbatical) to an entire month (if it was a year-long sabbatical) to prepare ourselves for engaging once again with the people, the ministry, and the working rhythms we left behind for a season. One of the reasons this aspect of our planning is so crucial is that we might return from sabbatical feeling so energized and refreshed that we do not pace ourselves, and before we know it we are back into the very schedule that left us so depleted in the first place! This means that *before* we leave on sabbatical we need to consider how we would like to reenter—who we would like to see and share with, how we would like to share and in what kind of setting, and how we would like to reconnect with individuals and our community as a whole. We can also give special attention to

187

those who provided the sabbatical and those who made sacrifices for it to be possible.

When I returned, I worked from the center out—first scheduling time with our board to share deeply with them my
learnings about and from sabbatical, and then time with our
staff. I did not see these connections as reporting as much as
they were an opportunity for sharing a spiritual conversation
with spiritual companions. I used my proposal as the structure
for sharing what I had experienced in each area, letting them
know what was good and what was hard. I was honest with
them about how happy I was *every single day* of my sabbatical,
and that it was a little scary to come back, even a little sad.

Having set my intention ahead of time to listen to God
deeply about my calling in the next season and also to listen
for anything God was saying to me about the Transforming
Center, we planned ahead to hold space for that along with
some important questions that surfaced in me on behalf of the
group and would provide shape for future conversations we
needed to have. All in all, the process of preparing to share with
the board as soon as possible when I got back was a really good
impetus for capturing what the sabbatical had been and
claiming the gifts of that time. And of course, it was meaningful
to have the opportunity to express deep gratitude as well.

I also scheduled one-on-one time right away with each
person who reports to me—to catch up on life, check in on how
their time went while I was away, to see what they had been
holding and what they needed from me now that I was back. It
was good for my soul to feel connected with people on a human,
intimate level before jumping back into the work. And my staff
was really wonderful about taking initiative to mark both the

beginning and the ending of my sabbatical in meaningful ways. It was good for them and good for me to know we had plans for reconnecting already on the calendar.

Since my first sabbatical I have learned that it is rather normal to experience a temporary but significant time of disorientation or depression during the first days and weeks after the renewal leave and that there may be a volatile range of emotions upon return. Knowing this, it is wise to go light on scheduling during the first week or two so that we are easing back in versus going from zero to sixty in the first few days back.

Finally, one of the best ways to prepare for reentry is to schedule a retreat with spiritual direction toward the end of our sabbatical time, to reflect on our experience, capture the learnings and insights God has given us, and think through any changes we want to make in the way we are living as a result of how God has worked in our life on sabbatical. Appendix B has some questions we can take into such a retreat time or into sessions with a spiritual director.

What Your Soul Wants to Say to God

What happened inside you as you read about sabbatical as a time of spiritual possibility? What are the emotions and visceral reactions (resonance and resistance) that you experienced, and to which of the opportunities were you most drawn?

Speak to God directly about this.

Work through the categories described in this chapter to determine if you feel drawn to incorporate any of them into your sabbatical planning, and how. Let this be an enjoyable opportunity for your soul to speak and say true things, without any forcing at all. If you are someone who does better processing out loud, set up a time to talk through these questions with a spiritually trusted person like a friend, spouse, or spiritual director.

- *Is there a spiritual practice you have been wanting to learn more about or experience more deeply? How can you build that into your sabbatical schedule?*

- *How might you deepen your attention to your inner life during sabbatical? Are there psychological issues/spiritual questions/questions for discernment you would like to attend to in the spaciousness of sabbatical time, and what kind of accompaniment are you willing to seek out—a spiritual director, therapist, spiritual friend, lectio divina group?*

- *How do you respond to the idea of keeping a sabbatical journal, and do you want to incorporate this as a practice?*

- *Is there anything related to your vocation, hobbies, and interests that you want to learn more about on sabbatical? What resources and opportunities are there for this?*

- *Are there any friends or relatives you want to be intentional about including in your sabbatical planning—people who are life-giving for you rather than work-related or life-draining? Brainstorm ways to make these connections happen.*

13

SETTING BOUNDARIES

● ● ◐

Those receiving sabbaticals have the responsibility to treat
them as a precious gift given by a loving congregation. A
sabbatical is not a vacation nor is it time away as much
as it is ministry—a ministry of the congregation to its
staff so that we may be all that God calls us to be.

RICHARD BULLOCK AND RICHARD BRUESEHOFF

THREE DAYS AFTER I officially left for my sabbatical, all hell broke loose in our country—literally. I had completed my work and officially unplugged on May 22, 2020, leaving town immediately as a way to drive a big "sabbatical stake" in the ground. On May 25, George Floyd was murdered by a White police officer who handcuffed him, pinned him to the ground, and pressed his knee into Floyd's neck for nine of the longest minutes we had ever witnessed. As the video of Floyd's death went viral and became the top news story in our country, major cities around the country and around the world exploded in protests, riots, fires, and looting. Even though a vast majority of protests were peaceful, there was also violence and vandalism breaking out everywhere; businesses that hadn't been vandalized yet were preemptively boarding up their doors and windows as people organized themselves to take their convictions and emotions into the streets. Our world was literally *on fire* and there I was— having finally gotten myself away and settled into sabbatical mode on the shores of Lake Michigan—glued to the television watching the unimaginable unfold before my very eyes.

Beyond the unbearable pain of witnessing this violent, humiliating, and racially motivated death, there was the greater pain of knowing that for my dearly beloved Black sisters and brothers this was nothing new. To them, seeing another Black body violated with impunity (at least for the moment) was alarmingly consistent with other forms of violence they have endured at the hands of White people throughout history. James Cone's classic work hammered me again with force, capturing the reality that what we had just witnessed was nothing less than a modern-day lynching:

> Lynching was the white community's way of forcibly reminding blacks of their inferiority and powerlessness. To be black meant that whites could do anything to you and your people, and that neither you nor anyone else could do anything about it. The Supreme Court Chief Justice Roger B. Taney had said clearly in the Dred Scott Decision (1857): blacks had no rights which the white man was bound to respect.

I was heartbroken. I paced. I wept. I called my friend Brenda so we could grieve and make meaning together. I couldn't

194

sleep, couldn't find peace, didn't know what I was supposed to do, being on sabbatical while the world burned. Finally, I just started writing—because that is the way I process things—and I wrote and wrote, pretty much uninterrupted for five or six days. What an amazing gift it was to have the freedom to write about what was bubbling up and to just stay with it. That freedom was part of what I had written into my sabbatical plan and I was grateful to be able to give this moment my whole attention.

STEWARDING THE GIFT

As I immersed myself in writing during those days, I did experience the "different kind of work" I have described already, carried out in a different way. Not only was I able to write, but I was able to carry what I was writing about in my heart and mind even when I wasn't writing. I ruminated, never having to fully leave my topic in order to focus on something else. Because there was no deadline, nor was I having to write with anyone else and their reactions in mind, I was able to think, read thoughtfully, reflect deeply, and just let the words pour out. And when the writing was done—if only for myself—I realized I had actually found some peace, because I had grappled spiritually with all that was happening, listened to God about it, and done the thing that was mine to do and not done the thing that was not mine to do.

But then the real question came: Would I put it out there—publish it—even though I was on sabbatical, everyone knew I was on sabbatical, and our whole organization was in a time of dormancy? It was painful to think that I and we in the Transforming Center would be silent at a time like this. Yet I knew I could not and would not do anything to violate the gift of sabbatical I had been given and the commitments we had all made to one another in creating a season of dormancy for our whole organization.

Because the situation in our country was so volatile and the question of whether or not justice would be done remained to be seen, I knew that anything we put out there would stir up responses—maybe even some good trouble—and we would need to be prepared to respond. But, of course, then *nobody* would be resting and my choice to post something on my blog would pull everyone out of dormancy.

You can see where God was taking me in all this, can't you? To a place of wrestling with boundaries. Sabbatical is a precious, precious gift that doesn't come around very often, so it needs boundaries to keep what is most important *in*, and what might be an interruption, distraction, or violation *out*. Just as sabbath-keeping involves being clear about what we will exclude so we can be very intentional about what we will include, sabbatical requires the same kind of thoughtful consideration. There are at least three areas where clear boundaries can be really important as we prepare for and then enter into sabbatical: work, technology, and relationships.

CEASING OUR WORK

Remember David Alves's clarification about the sabbath—the Hebrew word *shabbat,* used by God in Genesis, really means "stopping or ceasing," and thus what God calls us to do on our sabbath is to make an abrupt end to our *usual* labor. This nuance is really important to our understanding of sabbatical as well; it is an extended season of purposeful ceasing from our normal work and patterns in order to create space for planned rest and replenishment. This replenishment is more than just physical; it is mental, psychic, and spiritual. This means that the "work" of sabbatical is not only to rest but to purposefully engage in activities that are replenishing on all levels. The intention is not to sit around the whole time like a lump but rather to cease our normal labors in order to create space for that which is most *deeply* replenishing. Thus, an important question in preparing for sabbatical will be, What constitutes normal work for us, and how will we create boundaries that prevent us from getting drawn back in?

The fact that we have already learned how to set boundaries around sabbath will be very helpful because now we want to expand those boundaries to protect a bigger piece of the landscape.

One thing that really helps with boundaries is to have *a clear beginning and a clear ending* to our sabbatical, with rituals, if possible. Sabbatical should begin with a sending service or some other ritual that marks the fact that we are officially taking our hand off the plow, as well as a ritual for returning to our work and being received back into the community again as a co-laborer. Just as sabbath is a sanctuary in time, beginning and ending rituals around sabbatical help create this as a sanctuary in time as well. Of course, this means we must plan enough time for completing all that needs to be done before we leave so we can let go responsibly. We need to make sure we communicate clearly (verbally and in writing) who will do what and who has decision-making authority in different areas while we are gone. This may include duties like who will coordinate and do the preaching, teaching, and worship leading; who will oversee other aspects of ministry like youth, Christian education, and food pantry; who will run things operationally (finance, human resources, and anything having to do with building and grounds); and appointing a secretary or an administrative associate who is empowered to respond on our behalf to internal and external requests.

We may also want to leave a very short list of reasons why we *would* want to be contacted during our absence, mostly having to do with being informed about anything significant happening in the lives of our closest coworkers, such as a death in the family, serious illness, or something that necessitated a change in status. Making that clear can help us be at peace with letting go of our normal connectedness with people we care about; even though we will not be involved in planning or presiding over anything like funerals, weddings, and visitations while on sabbatical, we probably will want to show up and be present as a human being with our close ones if anything life altering should happen.

Generally, while a pastor is on sabbatical, all congregational duties like preaching, funerals, weddings, and visiting the sick should be done by others so we don't flip back into work and ministry mode. This might be hard in situations where we typically would be involved in planning, preaching, and visiting, but it can be a good thing if parishioners learn to let go and be less attached to the pastor they are accustomed to, instead receiving ministry from the very qualified persons who have been left in charge. This is actually an opportunity to practice and lean into the priesthood of all believers in a very concrete way. But it will take trust and humility—on our part and theirs. We will want to think this through *ahead of time* as part of planning, rather than waiting until the moment when something unexpected comes up and shock or other emotions cloud the issue.

The importance of being really clear about priorities and expectations, and maybe even structuring in some accountability for ourselves, cannot be overstated. Henri Nouwen's open struggle with boundaries on his sabbatical reminds us of our own struggle, illustrating just how important it is to mark out a clear and unambiguous path for ourselves as we enter into this important season. While Nouwen had been commissioned by his community "to say *no* to everything but writing," he seemed to do exactly the opposite! In one journal entry he describes a level of work and ministry that was very different from the stated purpose of his sabbatical.

> Most of the day I have been busy preparing for my ten-day trip that starts tomorrow—Newark, Chicago, San Francisco, Cleveland, Chicago, Newark. I am looking forward to several events: Don's birthday, visiting Jeff and Maurice, discussing the book of daily meditations with the publishers, a few days with Frank, Alvaro and Kevin, preaching at the installation of Jim in Cleveland, and leading a workshop about the inclusion of people with disabilities in the liturgy. It is going to be work as well as vacation.

Nouwen's struggle alerts us all to the fact that we must be ruthless in discerning how we are going to cease—really cease—our work and put good boundaries around this set-apart time. It also reminds us of just how important our community can be in helping us protect this time with loving boundaries. We might even appoint one person whom the leader going on sabbatical really trusts, to stay connected and check in every once in a while to support them in their intent. Sabbatical should not feel like punishment or exile. But I will say that, for me, the *love* of my community in giving me the gift of a sabbatical was one of the things God used to keep me within the guardrails we had all established. Since everyone around me had made such loving sacrifices in order for me to receive this gift, there was no way I was going to squander it by letting work bleed into it. I was determined to honor their gift by receiving it fully.

DISCERNING RELATIONAL BOUNDARIES

All of this points to the fact that we need to consider relational boundaries on sabbatical as well. We all have some relationships that are life-giving and others that feel like work or that create stress and anxiety. On sabbatical we should feel very free to limit contact with people who drain our energies—unless God is clearly inviting us to be intentional about using the energy we are gaining from resting to attend to important relationships we might have neglected or that need more time and space. Choosing to use our energy in this way should, for the most part, apply only to family and friends—not colleagues from work. This is an extremely important distinction that needs to be discerned.

I intentionally chose to give good energy and focus to some relationship-tending within my extended family following my dad's death; this was carefully planned and it was one of the things I wanted to do from a more rested and spacious place. I will be forever grateful that it even occurred to me to use sabbatical as an opportunity to make this kind of investment. At the same time, there were other relationships that I was careful not to include because they were too much work and would have cost more than I was able to give.

There is an invitation here to be thoughtful and intentional about what relationships we will allow in during our sabbatical time, rather than inadvertently getting caught up in situations with people who do not contribute to our resting or are outside the priorities we have identified for this set-apart time.

TAMING OUR TECHNOLOGY

Related to all of this is the need to tame our technology so it works *for* us in support of sabbatical priorities and not against us. Technology is neutral—not good or bad—but it is our intentionality around what we do and don't do with it that makes it good or bad for us. Our increasing addiction to technology and the convenience of being able to access email and news from anywhere and everywhere at all times of the day and night makes unplugging an almost unmanageable proposition that is even more challenging on sabbatical.

To state the obvious, we need to make sure we unplug completely from work email—and I would go so far as to suggest we actually turn off access to it—so we are not tempted to briefly check in. Putting a "vacation responder" message on our email informing people about the dates of our sabbatical and who they can contact for whatever they need is a courtesy to them, and it also frees us up, knowing that we won't leave people wondering why we have not responded. And we will also be freed up knowing that anyone who contacts us will be able to find a way forward with their question or issue by contacting others. We can make sure family and friends can find us with a personal email address given only to those to whom we are closest.

Depending on how much access people have to our cell-phones for work purposes, we may also want to consider recording an "out of office" message on that phone and putting it away while securing another phone for use on sabbatical. That way we can give a personal phone number to those we want to be in touch with during sabbatical, but no one else will be able to reach us with items that hijack our rest and catapult us back into work mode. This is a small price to pay for the benefit of being unreachable and unavailable for work-related interruptions.

I did not do either of these things, and I wish I had. At one point early on in my sabbatical, I realized I was only quasi-unplugged and that I needed to cut deeper into my patterns with technology so I could truly rest and not risk being hijacked by messages from the outside world. When I started my sabbatical, I felt like my internal boundaries were so weak that anything that could unsettle me did—getting me all riled up emotionally about what was going on in the world, questions that had no easy answers, and my own leadership impulse to try and *do* something, anything.

As I let go into this precious time and started to be more in touch with my human being rather than my human doing, it was like I lost a tough outer skin and became more aware of a fragile, tender inner self that simply needed care and protection. It took a while to realize I needed the help of external boundaries to keep my internal guardrails in place so I could keep sinking and settling into where I needed to be—with God in the depths of my being. I needed to create a womb of sorts—a protected place where my soul could feel safe from the onslaught of all that comes at us in the world. So at some point I gave myself permission to unsubscribe from *everything* to further protect a womb-like environment where I was claiming more of a sense of agency about what I would let in, as opposed to letting the world push its agenda on me. My sensitive soul needed to be more protected during this time, and giving this to myself resulted in a capacity to keep going deeper and deeper into what God had for me. I knew I could resubscribe to anything I chose when I returned, but mostly I just didn't.

ENTERING THE COCOON

On sabbatical, we spin a cocoon around ourselves—a protected place for dis-integration in order to find re-integration eventually. It is oddly disintegrating for a leader to stop doing all the things that seem to define them; most leaders over-identify with the leader aspect of themselves, including the compulsion to be culturally relevant and culturally engaged. In the transformation of the caterpillar into a butterfly, there is a stage when the tiny little being disintegrates into a primordial, soupy mess—trusting some instinctual knowing that this is not the end but a new beginning. But that doesn't make the disintegration any less alarming and uncomfortable. It does feel dark in a way, but also darkly comforting to be out of the public view so we don't have to present ourselves as being put together, so we can be in pieces (the very definition of disintegrated), trusting ourselves to God and God's timing in putting us back together.

It seems to me that this is another way of talking about Henri Nouwen's idea of fashioning our own desert: "What needs to be guarded is the life of the Spirit within us." There needs to be some real intentionality and a certain vigilance brought to this based on what we know about ourselves. Here are some questions to help us think this through:

- What is it in the external world that gets me emotionally riled up?
- What is it that routinely distracts me from knowing what my soul needs to say to God and then trying to say it?
- What kinds of things tend to pull me into other people's agendas for me and away from what God knows I need and is trying to invite me into?
- What relationships, activities, social media platforms, or news outlets cause my soul to skitter back into hiding because it doesn't feel safe or free?

On sabbatical, unlike most other seasons, we have a real invitation from God to back away from the inner dynamics of worry and strife stirred up by the external distractions of too much news and compulsive engagement with social media. But this is not easy and there will always be challenges. Which brings me back to the struggle I was having at the beginning of my sabbatical.

TRUSTING GOD TO RUN THE WORLD?

It's pretty clear that writing for publication and interacting with publishers about writing projects constitutes work for me; I know myself well enough to understand that writing with the intent to publish—even brainstorming writing projects—is so stimulating that it takes me right out of resting mode. Even though I know plenty of people who use sabbatical to take on or complete writing projects, this was off the table for me, given the clarity we all had about the purpose of my sabbatical. But, as I described earlier, this commitment was severely tested at the beginning of my sabbatical.

As the racial crisis in the United States continued to intensify in the summer of 2020, I was so uncomfortable about both options—remaining silent or putting something out for publication—that I reached out to board members who were available, asking that we discern this together. It turned out we could not find agreement on the question of whether publishing a blog post would violate my sabbatical, and because we had decided that my sabbatical would provide a period of dormancy for our whole organization, no one else was supposed to be publishing anything either! Several board members were on vacation, so we couldn't even pull everyone together to discuss it thoroughly without violating their time away.

Those of us who were able to convene found ourselves caught on the horns of a dilemma—on the one hand, we had already determined that writing for publication constitutes work for me, not to mention the fact that it would stir up comments and a need to be responding on social media. On the other hand, what we were in the midst of as a culture was turning into the most important moment in the civil rights movement since the 1960s; *everybody* was writing, making statements, and pontificating about it. How could I and our organization not be a part of this moment and stand publicly with our Black brothers and sisters?

This whole situation was crazy hard and very confusing, so I reached out to Phaedra Blocker, one of our board members, for an offline conversation to see how she was feeling about it all. In particular, I wanted to talk to her about the slogan "Silence is violence" that was showing up in protests, and ask her to speak to me from *within* the Black community about whether or not the Transforming Center would be put in the category of being complicit through our silence if we didn't speak out right this minute. Ever the pragmatist, her response was painful but true and helped me to find peace. With a deep sigh she said,

> This moment does feel different from other moments and I pray that it is. But you also need to realize that what is happening right now is nothing new for us in the Black community. We are used to it. And here's the thing . . . everyone close to us knows you and we are not silent on issues of racial justice; we address it in every community we lead, and we are planning to do more. There are so many people writing and making statements right now I'm not sure anyone can really take much more. This issue is going to still be here when you get back. And maybe if you wait, it will be a better time anyway for people to hear from you.

What she was saying rang a bell that was consistent with a statement one of my teachers, Gerald May, often made—that with God there are no emergencies. In other words, God was not surprised by what was happening or the timing. In fact, God knew it was going to happen, and knew I would be on sabbatical and that the Transforming Center would be dormant when it did. Shocking as it may seem, somehow God was prepared to handle it without me and somehow the world would find its way through this part of the crisis without hearing from me until I emerged from the place God had called me to be.

HE'S GOT THE WHOLE WORLD IN HIS HANDS

This was probably the most challenging moment of my entire sabbatical experience and I am glad we got it over with early. While a case could have been made for handling this situation in several different ways, I found the most peace in (1) honoring our board's lack of unity on the question (and even our lack of ability to convene) and remaining faithful to our original, God-ordained commitment to this season of dormancy, and (2) dropping into a deeper place of trust that God could run the world without me while I remained faithful to what God had invited me into. It seems silly to say it like that, but it is true.

I was reminded of Henri Nouwen's classic work, *In the Name of Jesus*, in which he describes the three temptations of Jesus and how those apply to Christian leadership. The first temptation he names is the temptation to be relevant: "Turn these stones into bread" (Matthew 4:3). In other words, the temptation is to take a shortcut to meet immediate needs rather than staying true to one's true vocation and mission—which for me in this moment was to embrace my humanness and rest myself in God. My sabbatical was forcing me to do what Nouwen's life among those with learning disabilities had forced him to do, and that was "to let go of my relevant self—the self that can do things, show things, build things—and forced me to reclaim that unadorned self in which I am completely vulnerable, open to receive and give love regardless of any accomplishments."

As I wrestled to let go of my relevant self, I felt God teaching me gently about another kind of rest, one that I had not yet discovered—rest from a leader's calling to be actively engaged with the world and its issues. When we are in our normal work and leadership mode, we are actively engaged in being in God

207

for the world, and rightly so. We carry the suffering of our world and its people and our own flock on our shoulders. But when we are on sabbatical the mandate is different—it is to *dis*engage from active involvement with the world and its issues, and to practice trust that God really can take care of God's world without our direct active involvement when ceasing is what we have been called to do.

I say *active* involvement because, of course, we will still be involved through our prayers. But we will be challenged to believe—really believe—that our prayers matter, that being in God's presence on behalf of others, even when it is not our responsibility to take action, *really does make a difference.* Furthermore, it is a call to trust that God can and will carry out God's purposes through others who are in a different season than we are—for example, those not on sabbatical at the moment. What a wonderful opportunity to live and practice the truth that it is through the whole body of Christ on the earth that the will of God will be done and God's kingdom will come; it is never up to one member of the body to do it all.

WHEN GOD REACHES FOR US

All of this is humbling, but true, for those of us accustomed to thinking of ourselves as relevant and therefore indispensable, or as indispensable *because* we are so relevant. Maybe one of the best things we can do on sabbatical is to just go ahead and let the humbling begin. These lines from a poem by Rainer Maria Rilke touch on this:

Through the empty branches the sky remains. . . .
Be the ground lying under that sky.

Be modest now, like a thing,
Ripened until it is real,
So that he who began it all
Can find you when he reaches for you.

So I ask you this: Is there anything more significant during sabbatical than to become more real, more human, so that when God reaches for us we can be found? So much of the time we act as if—and maybe even believe—all of our doing is what makes us real. But on sabbatical we learn that to become more real is to ripen and settle into that modest thing called our humanity; we learn to put some good boundaries around this way of being so we are, quite simply, ready and available when God reaches for us and touches us. And because for once we are not moving so fast and we are not so driven to distraction by self-aggrandizement, we are able to fully receive whatever that touch brings.

What Your Soul Wants to Say to God

Take some time now to respond to God about what you are thinking and feeling in response to the boundaries described here—boundaries around your work, your relationships, your technologies. What resonated? What do you resist? What seems hard but good and right?

What do you want to give your attention to on sabbatical? What boundaries will need to be put in place in order for you to bring this attention? Say it to God in your own words.

Begin to list out the boundaries you want to put in place in order to protect this most precious season. Be as concrete as possible.

Interlude

A BLESSING *for* SABBATICAL TIME

FROM THE COMMUNITY, FOR THE ONE
RECEIVING SABBATICAL

• • •

OPENING

Oh God, make speed to save us!

Oh Lord, make haste to help us!

**A MEDITATION ON PSALM 46:10
(FROM HENRI NOUWEN)**

Be still and know that I am God.

Be still. Be quiet. Be silent. Be tranquil. Be present. Be now.
Be here.

The first task of the disciple is to be with the Lord, to sit at his
feet, to listen, and to be attentive to all he says, does, and asks.

Our Lord is all we need and want. Our stronghold, our refuge,
our shepherd, our wisdom. God cares for us, feeds us, gives
us life.

Be still and know that I am God.

To be still is hard. It means to let God speak to us, breathe in
us, act in us, pray in us. Let God enter into the most hidden
parts of our being.

God touch us even where it may hurt us and cause us pain. To be still is to trust, to surrender, to let go, to have faith.

Be still and know that I am God.

Be still. God is and God acts. Not once in a while, not on special occasions, but all the time.

Be still and listen to the one who speaks to you always, feel the actions of the one who acts always, and taste the presence of the one who is present always.

Know. Come to know real knowledge, full intimate knowing.

A form of diagnosis, a knowing through and through. A knowing with the heart, a knowing by heart. Be still and know. Come to that still knowledge.

There is a very restless knowledge, a confusing, distracting, dividing knowledge. But knowing God is a knowing of the heart, of the whole person. It is a knowing that is also seeing, hearing, touching, smelling.

Be still and know that I am God.

That is not meant to be a fearful knowledge, but a peaceful knowledge. God is not a God of the dead, but a God of the living. God is not a revengeful God, but a God of love.

Know that I am God, your God. The God who is only love, the God who touches you with his limitless and unconditional love.

Be still and know that I love you.

That I hold you in the palm of my hand. That I have counted the hairs of your head. That you are the apple of my eye. That your name is written in my heart. "Do not be afraid . . . it is I."

There is nothing in us that needs to be hidden from God's love. Our guilt, our shame, our fear, our sins. He wants to see it, touch it, heal it, and make himself known. There is no other God than the Lord of Love.

Be still and know that I am God.

God is not in the storm, nor in the earthquake, nor in fire, but in the still, small voice, the gentle breeze, and the sheer silence.

Be still and know that I am God. Take these words with you in the week to come. Let them be like a little seed planted in the good soil of your heart and let them grow.

Be still and know that I am God.

SILENCE

PRAYER FOR GOD'S BLESSING

Leader: O Holy One, we bring [person's name] before you, our [sister/brother] in Christ, our leader and friend. We send [her/him] on sabbatical with our earnest prayers, asking your blessing upon [her/him], and upon [congregation/ministry name] while [she/he] is away.

All: May this sabbatical be a time of quiet excitement in you. May [her/his] rest be deep and rich. May [her/his] mind be clear and focused. May this season of rest in you be full of consolation.

Leader: Guide [her/his] steps, O God. May [she/he] know your accompanying presence each day and find you ready and longing to be with [her/him].

All: In these months away, may [she/he] enjoy a release from leadership responsibilities, a childlike curiosity, and a thorough refreshment of body, mind, and spirit.

Leader: Grant to [her/him], we pray, times of reading, times of play, times of deep contemplation, of rich conversation, of both leisurely dreaming and focused reflection. And enable [her/him] to gaze in wonder at the beauty of your creation.

All: Guard [her/him], O God, from discouragement and loneliness. Shield [her/him] from the evil one.

Leader: Hear your servant when [she/he] prays to you, Holy God. Help [her/him] to worship you freely, whether in multitude or in solitude, joy or sorrow, in strength or in weakness. Watch over [her/him], and draw [her/him] close to yourself.

All: And for those of us who will hold responsibility for tending the work of the [congregation/ministry] while [she/he] is away, O God, grant us wisdom, discernment, insight, and passion.

Leader: Accomplish your purposes among us, O God. Tune our hearts to the voice of your Spirit. Wake us to be present to you and to one another in the tasks that are ours to do. And now we seek a word of counsel and blessing.

From the one who is departing: Beloved, hear these words from the apostle Paul, to God's people in Corinth. Let them be my word to you as well. "And that's about it, friends. Be cheerful. Keep things in good repair. Keep your spirits up. Think in harmony. Be agreeable. Do all that, and the God of love and peace will be with you for sure. The amazing grace of the Master, Jesus Christ, the extravagant love of God, the intimate friendship of the Holy Spirit, be with you all" (from 2 Corinthians 13:11, 14, *The Message*).

All: For your sake, O God, guard us all from the evil one, that your plans for this sabbatical may not be altered, but will be accomplished according to your will and power.

Leader: Through Christ, and in the power of the Holy Spirit, we pray. Amen.

EPILOGUE

SAVED BY REST

Rest in not the reward of our liberation,
nor something we lay hold of once we are free.
It is the path that delivers us there.

COLE ARTHUR RILEY

THERE IS A QUOTE in Jewish literature that says, "More than Israel has kept Shabbat, Shabbat has kept Israel." This resonates with me, because of all the spiritual practices, sabbath is the one that has *kept me*. Even when I have not kept sabbath very well—when I have cheated (myself, really) by doing a little work, "just glancing" at my technologies, looking for loopholes that enable me to make progress on *something* during sabbath time when I should be resting—the promise of sabbath, the principles of sabbath rest, and the gift of sabbatical have *kept me*. They have kept me from ruining myself and others on the treadmill of stress, exhaustion, and pushing beyond what human beings are built for.

As human beings we are constantly looking for rest. And it's not just more and better sleep we are looking for, as important as that is; we are desperately seeking rest for our minds, a reprieve from the intensity of our thoughts and emotions, and replenishment of all that gets taken from us in our engagement with a very demanding world. As humbling as it is to admit, we cannot keep going and going and going. We get tired and we need to stop. Sabbath is God's way of showing us that we are allowed to—and then showing us how.

If there is one verse in Scripture that sums up the power of sabbath rest in just a few words, it is this familiar verse in Isaiah: "In returning and rest you shall be saved; in quietness and in trust shall be your strength" (Isaiah 30:15). It is a great verse taken out of context, but it's an even better verse taken *in* context because it describes the obstacles we face in saying yes to this invitation. So, have you ever wondered what God was really saying here, and to whom, and what it actually means? Return to what? Saved from what? How exactly does rest save us? Let's close our reflections on sabbath by meditating on Isaiah 30 where, in the midst of God's invitation to rest, the Israelites and their resistance are described in ways that are eerily similar to our own.

People who carry out a plan, but not mine (Isaiah 30:1). When was the last time you made a plan or got involved in a plan because it represented something you wanted or it made sense to you, but you didn't even ask God about it? How did this happen and what was the outcome? Are you caught in jobs and plans and projects that keep you from returning and resting, and is there any way you can get out? What would need to change in your life in order to enter into the sabbath rest God is not just offering, but commanding—for our good?

One of the ways churches and communities find ourselves in this position is that we keep adding more church services

216

and ministry initiatives that keep pastors, staff, and volunteers working seven days a week, without giving any thought to how these additions make sabbath-keeping impossible. The ideas for "more" always seem strategic—of course they do!—but how does implementing them affect our ability to live into the rhythms of work and rest God is offering us? Did we ask God about it when we were putting these plans in place and then really listen for his response, or did we just think our way into them? Hopefully we are asking these questions of ourselves in private moments with God, and hopefully there are those in our leadership groups who ask questions about how adding more programs will affect everyone's ability to establish and maintain sane rhythms of work and rest. Maybe that person is you!

People who make an alliance, but against my will (Isaiah 30:1). This phrase is talking about who and what we align ourselves with; it is talking about partnerships and who or what we are allowing to influence our thinking and our priorities. I remember one young leader who was very entrepreneurial and chose to align himself with a business venture that required being available 24-7—at least in the beginning. It involved selling really hard and always being "on" and available to anyone interested in his product. Saying yes to this opportunity, as lucrative as it was, robbed him and his family of the sabbath pattern he and his wife were trying to uphold within their family. Until he shed that alignment, it was not possible for him to fully enter into the sabbath rest his heart longed for.

People who set out to go down to Egypt, to take refuge in the protection of Pharaoh, to seek shelter in the shadow of Egypt, without asking for my counsel (Isaiah 30:2). Or to express it another way, "putting [our] trust in oppression and deceit, and rely[ing] on them" (v. 12). These verses allude to the many times when the Israelites gave in to their fear that God's provision would not be enough, moments when embracing the freedoms of a sabbath life felt so new and uncertain that they were tempted to go back to old and familiar ways of feeling secure. For the Israelites, this temptation was captured in their cry, "If only we had died by the hand of the Lord in the land of Egypt, when we sat by the fleshpots and ate our fill of bread" (Exodus 16:3).

I experience this temptation to "cheat" just a little bit by trying to get some work done on the sabbath, attempting to "get ahead of email" by checking once or twice, writing a few paragraphs on a book or an article I am authoring, reading books related to my work that take me back into "thinking really hard about things" like I often do during the workweek. Now I recognize these choices as going back to old ways of feeling secure by being productive and getting more done rather than staying in my discomfort in God's presence and trusting God with my life. When I give in to such temptations, the only person I cheat is myself, because I take myself out of resting mode rather than trusting God to multiply the work I accomplish in six days and make it enough.

"People . . . who say to the seers, 'Do not see,' and to the prophets, 'Do not prophesy to us what is right; speak to us smooth things, prophesy illusions, leave the way, turn aside from the path, let us hear no more about the Holy One of Israel'" (Isaiah 30:9-11). These verses speak to all the ways we seek to avoid the hard word and the unsettling truths about the way we are living, the path we are taking, and where it will eventually lead. In the end, our busyness and 24-7 lifestyles function as a way of making sure we do not hear the wise ones

in our lives and may even silence the voice of God himself. We all have subtle and not-so-subtle ways of shutting down the voices we would rather not hear, the voices (including the still, small Voice of God) that would challenge us toward deeper levels of spiritual transformation. But when we rest from the noise, the busyness, the drivenness, and all that typically distracts us, there is the promise that we will hear the voice of our teacher saying, "This is the way; walk in it" (Isaiah 30:21).

A DEEPER KNOWING

And this brings us to one final blessing of sabbath-keeping. Invariably, during sabbath time, God impresses a deeper knowing on our souls—sometimes that might be guidance we have been seeking that seems to come "out of the blue," it may be a challenge to our values, to the way we are living, or some aspect of our false self. Maybe it's an affirmation of something that is deeply true and good in ourselves that we've lost touch with, or just a sense of how deeply loved and valued we are. Maybe it's an inexplicable feeling of empowerment for the week ahead as true, life-giving energy flows back into us and God reaffirms our calling to the work he has given us. Whatever it is, the practice of returning and resting is a powerful antidote to our very human tendency to protect and live out of our illusions rather than hearing God's word to us.

Returning to a practice and a posture of resting *in* God's provision through a sabbath once a week and a sabbatical every seventh year provides a routine way of stepping off the treadmill of our nonstop lives before we get thrown off and injured very badly. Resting *with* God in what has been given while trusting that it is enough is a profoundly transforming experience—especially since it has to do with quieting our human striving, cultivating peace by dropping into a place of deep trust, and fostering contentment with gratitude. If you think about it, quietness and trust, peace and contentment, gratitude and thanksgiving are all hallmarks of a deeply spiritual life, and we cannot will them into being. But what we can do is allow God to form these character traits in us through a practice that fosters returning to a centered and grounded place in the life God has given us.

Something happens on the sabbath that I cannot explain. Something is *formed in me* that I cannot force through my own effort or will. These lines from one of Wendell Berry's sabbath poems capture something of the mystery of it all:

The mind that comes to rest is tended
In ways that it cannot intend:
Is borne, preserved, and comprehended
By what it cannot comprehend.

On the sabbath we encounter a God who has been waiting for us—waiting to be gracious to us and show mercy to us—in ways we cannot always fully perceive. It is a means of grace through which God does something in us and for us that we cannot do for ourselves, nor would we even know to do it. "Your Sabbath, Lord, thus keeps us by your will, not ours," Berry goes on to say, which puts sabbath-keeping solidly in the category of an essential spiritual practice that opens us to God's transforming work. It is a form of sweet surrender in which we find ourselves in God week by week—no matter how lost we have become—until this strong and steady rhythm carries us all the way to the shores of the eternal rest God has waiting for us.

GRATITUDE

MY GRATITUDE IS FIRST TO GOD, who thought to give his beloved children a gift as loving and well chosen as the sabbath. How could you not love a God like that?

And then my gratitude goes to the authors who struggled, as I have done, to put the beauty and the meaning, the challenge and the invitation, of sabbath into words. Wayne Muller, Abraham Heschel, Walter Brueggemann, Wendell Berry, Tilden Edwards . . . your voices kept calling to me until I was ready to order my life to receive this great gift.

To the communities who have explored and practiced with me: To my family—who first tolerated and then leaned into my early experimentations with sabbath-keeping. To the Transforming Center staff who have followed me gladly into this practice to the extent that I can confidently say we are a sabbath community. Thank you for rallying around my sabbatical seasons and caring so lovingly for the Transforming Center when I have been away.

To the Transforming Center board who granted me my first sabbatical and took responsibility for raising the funds to support it—Jimmy Lee, Jonathan Taylor Haley, Vicki Degner, Phaedra Blocker, B. J. Woodworth, David Hughes. Your generosity stirred me deeply and gave me a gift that changed my life.

To all who have shared their sabbath and sabbatical experiences with me and with the readers of this book. Your stories carry this work beyond my own personal experience to a more universal reality—demonstrating that there are so many ways to practice and so many ways to benefit.

To Fr. Ron Rolheiser who is not only one of my respected teachers but has become a true friend. Thank you for standing with me in this work.

To my sabbath friend, Brenda Salter McNeil. How many sabbath conversations have we shared where, in each other's company, we were able to say that true thing our souls needed to say to God? Too many to count. . . . And to Linda Richardson for being such a loving spiritual companion throughout my sabbatical time.

To my faithful editor, Cindy Bunch, at InterVarsity Press. The care and attention you give to the editorial process instills within me the courage to keep sending my babies out into the world.

And to my husband, Christopher, who continues to be my most intimate partner in wrestling with the implications and invitations of sabbath-keeping. Many times the sabbath has saved *us*—enabling us to bring our best selves to each other and to the life we share. As Wayne Muller says, "The world aches for the generosity of a well-rested people." Time and time again we have been able to bring the generosity of our more rested selves to each other on the sabbath and I look forward to it week by week.

And now, "Praise God from whom all blessings flow"— especially the blessing of the sabbath.

A SABBATH WORKSHEET

BASED ON YOUR DESIRE and the particulars of your situation, decide on a day you will try one sabbath. Use the following categories to start making plans and preparations for setting aside work, worry, consumerism, and reliance on technology in order to enter into the rest of God.

- *Consider what you will exclude.* What activities related to work, buying and selling, worry, and technology will you set aside so this day is truly a day of ceasing your work and resting, remembering, and delighting? What scheduling choices will need to be made regarding the other six days in order to set aside the seventh as a day of rest?

- *Consider what you will include.* What activities bring delight and how will you incorporate them? Include activities that *rest and delight the body* (a nap, a walk in the woods, a bike ride, a long bubble bath, a bask in the rays of the sun or in the shade of a beautiful tree, a meal comprised of your favorite foods and friends or family to share it with, making love in the afternoon); *rest the mind and replenish the spirit* (art, music, reading for pleasure, playing with children, spending time with a good friend who enlivens you); and *restore the soul* (worship in community, family rituals or shared activities that create a spirit of reverence for God, additional time for silence, prayer, journaling that helps you to reflect on God's presence during the past week). Be realistic about the stage of life your family is in, and if you have young children consider some of the ideas found in appendix B to make it doable and enjoyable to be together as a family in this way. If you are in college or live alone, consider whether there are any others with whom you would like to share a communal meal or some other part of the day.

- *Practical considerations.* Do not plan your sabbath too precisely, make it too structured, or pack it too full of activity. Allow for spaciousness and flexibility and at the same time think through important details like when you will go to church, who else you might include in your day, anything new or creative you would like to try. And when sabbath comes, give yourself the day to feel what it's like to wake up and know this is a day of rest, replenishment, and delight. Put the day you have chosen on your calendar and pray that God will help you honor this sabbath and keep it holy. Then just see where it leads you.

Note: If you are a pastor, on a pastoral staff team, or a volunteer, and pulling off the church service is part of your paid work or you carry a lot of responsibility, you may feel like you're always "on." Consider starting sabbath time after church and extend it through the evening and through the next morning, or even through noon on Monday if possible. At the very least, I suggest all church staff teams take twenty-four hours "off" from the time of the last church service. Arrange for a receptionist to handle calls or to connect with an on-call pastor if a need arises that can't be put off until the pastoral staff is back.

PREPARING *for* REENTRY

GATHERING UP THE GIFTS OF SABBATICAL

ONE WAY TO BRING GOOD CLOSURE to sabbatical before reentering your life in ministry is to schedule a spiritual retreat, extended time in solitude, and/or time with a spiritual director to "gather up" the gifts contained within your sabbatical. Such gifts may be something as broad and overarching as revisiting and clarifying your sense of God's call on your life for the next season, or something as practical as how you will schedule the rhythms going forward—your rule of life. (For a full description of a rule of life, see Ruth Haley Barton, *Sacred Rhythms*.) If you already have one, this is a really good time to take a look at your rule of life to see if it still holds or if changes need to be made.

In particular, if you did not have a sabbath practice before taking sabbatical, or if your practice had slipped, coming back from sabbatical is an ideal time to renew your commitment to this. It's also a good time to begin other spiritual practices God is impressing on your heart or that you experienced to be particularly fruitful and life-giving on sabbatical.

Here are some questions and areas of reflection to spend time with as you approach reentry:

- Pull out your sabbatical proposal and reflect on each of the areas you listed as needs or desires. Reflect on what happened in those areas and jot down notes and reflections.

- What was good and went well on your sabbatical? What was hard and what do you wish might have gone differently?

- What did you learn about yourself on sabbatical? How do you want to bring this back to your life in leadership?

- What were the questions you brought into sabbatical and what did God say to you about them?

- What spiritual practices were most meaningful to you on sabbatical? How can you incorporate at least some of that as you resume your normal life? Are there any needed changes to make to your schedule and life patterns going forward?

- What surprised you on sabbatical? What delighted you?

- What is a favorite story from sabbatical? (You may want to capture this in writing.)

- Is there any physical symbol or icon of this sabbatical season that you want to bring into your space to remind you of what God did during this time and who God was to you? Any special Scripture you can claim from this time?

- Are there any thank-you notes or other expressions of gratitude that you don't want to miss as you return?

- What is your sense of calling as you emerge from this time?

BECOMING *a* SABBATH COMMUNITY

A CONVERSATION GUIDE FOR GROUPS

BECOMING A SABBATH COMMUNITY will require unity, shared desire, and practical intent. This guide is intended to open up conversations with your family or church, ministry organization or business, as you order your life together around sane rhythms of work and rest. Such conversations can create space for your community to grapple with practical issues in order to identify a path forward, and can be used in all kinds of groups—Sunday school classes and Christian education settings, small groups and house churches, boards and staff teams, families and spiritual friendships.

The purpose of these conversations is not to convince but to offer an opportunity for meaningful interaction around matters of great importance to us all—the quality and pace of our lives guided by God's presence. Then, as God leads, participants may be able to agree together on practical steps to take together. Ideally, each person participating will have their own copy of this book and will be committed to reading the assigned portions prior to each discussion, taking time to respond personally in the "What Your Soul Wants to Say to God" section of each chapter. It may be helpful to read with a highlighter in hand, noting places of desire and longing, resonance, resistance, or need for further exploration.

Before you begin the group experience, take time to establish a clear purpose for your times together, articulated in a way that makes sense and is compelling to all. Establish some basic guidelines for how you will interact together. *Do not take for granted that people know how to listen and interact in ways that are spiritually fruitful.* Most of us are much more skilled at arguing and trying to prove our own point than we are at engaging in mutually influencing relationships. Following are suggestions for listening and interacting during these conversations.

1. *At the beginning of each session, take time to become settled in God's presence*—a prayer inviting God's guidance, a few moments in silence, a lectio divina experience with Scripture, a reflective reading of a passage from the book, a poem, or some other related resource.

2. *Listen to others* with your entire self (senses, feelings, intuition, imagination, and rational faculties), seeking to understand where they are coming from and how what they are saying makes sense in their context. *Listen to yourself* and take responsibility for what is happening inside you; if you feel uncomfortable, defensive, or argumentative, be curious about what that says about you versus projecting it onto others.

3. *Do not interrupt* as others are sharing, and resist the temptation to formulate what you want to say while someone else is speaking.

4. *Pause between speakers* to give group members a chance to absorb what has been said.

5. *Make "I" statements.* Speak for yourself only, expressing your own thoughts and feelings, referring to your own experiences or testimonies that others have entrusted to you that might benefit the conversation. Avoid being hypothetical or merely conceptual or theological. Steer away from making broad generalizations, and keep the conversation practical.

6. *Ask questions* that enable you to wonder about things together. Do not challenge what others say, but instead express curiosity and a desire to understand.

7. *Respect each person's journey with God.* Believe the best, trusting that God is active in their lives and that their journey is taking place at God's initiative and under God's guidance.

8. *Leave space for others to speak.* Pay attention to the group as a whole—to those who have spoken aloud as well as to those who haven't. If you notice that someone hasn't spoken or seems uncomfortable, feel free to ask them directly what they are thinking. Some people aren't as comfortable as others with asserting themselves in conversation, but when space is created for them to speak, they have much to offer because they have been listening and observing quietly. If someone seems to have shut down, gently ask them about it. Leave space for anyone who may want to speak a first time before speaking a second time yourself.

9. *Hold your desires and opinions—even your convictions— lightly.* Be willing to be influenced by others you respect and who have been given to you for this journey.

10. *Assure people that they always have the option to say "I pass"* if they do not feel comfortable sharing about a particular question.

If members of your group follow these guidelines even some of the time, you will do well! And one more thing . . . do not rush. There are no emergencies with God. This group guide is offered in six sessions, but if you find need for more than one meeting per session, feel free to take an extra week anytime. For instance, going over the conversation guidelines and sharing sabbath stories may be all you have time for in the first session—you may need an extra session to complete the rest of the questions.

SESSION 1 (READ AND REFLECT ON CHAPTERS 1 AND 2)

Settle in and invite God's presence through prayer, shared silence, lectio divina with Scripture, or a reflective reading.

1. Invite each person to share their own sabbath story and reflect on it a bit. This will take time—maybe the whole time!—and it will be important for group members to receive each other's stories and experiences with reverence for their journey. At the end of each person's sharing, thank them without judgment or making evaluative statements. Feel free to ask clarifying questions in order to understand where people are coming from. If you do not have significant experience with sabbath-keeping, simply describe what you do know about it, how you feel about it right now in terms of openness, resistance, etc. Share whatever history you have (or don't have) with sabbath.

2. Where did you find yourself experiencing your own longing or desire, need or even desperation as you read?

3. What do you think about the idea that sabbath begins with God, versus being a practice having to do with one ethnic group? What difference (if any) does it make to think about sabbath as a way of *participating with God* in God's very nature?

4. Discuss the idea that "the beauty is in the rhythm" (p. 23). How have you experienced the dynamic of rest giving meaning to work and vice versa?

5. Is there anything God is stirring up in you to explore or try as a result of reading these chapters?

Close with silent space for people to listen to what their soul wants to say to God, and then express that in spoken prayers. After a brief time, the convener of the group can close with simple words of prayer that gather up the desires expressed by the group, affirming that God has been present and heard those desires.

SESSION 2 (READ AND REFLECT ON CHAPTERS 3 AND 4)

Settle in and invite God's presence through prayer, shared silence, lectio divina with Scripture, or a reflective reading.

1. Have you ever had an experience like the one described at the beginning of chapter three—one you might describe as a wake-up call? What was that like and how have you responded?

2. How do you respond to the idea that sabbath is about resisting the forces of culture and being liberated from

oppression? Does it shift anything in the way you view sabbath?

3. How do you experience the "potent combination" of cultural patterns of consumerism and relentless productivity, plus personal drivenness, as described on pages 30-31? Talk with each other about any sense of being in bondage in this way. Let yourself envision what it might look like to practice sabbath as a way of resisting and practicing freedom.

4. Do you agree or disagree with the idea that sabbath is the great equalizer versus a day off for the rich and famous? What would it take for more people to have equal opportunity to experience sabbath in our culture today?

5. As you think of sabbath as a communal discipline versus one that people are trying to figure out all by themselves, do you feel you have had the encouragement, guidance, and support of your community, or do your community's patterns make this difficult in any way?

6. How does knowing that sabbath is not the same thing as solitude and silence affect your sabbath practice?

7. If you are a leader of any kind of community (including your family community), what do you perceive is your role in cultivating a sabbath community? What needs to take place in your personal journey in order for you to lead authentically?

SESSION 3 (READ AND REFLECT ON CHAPTERS 5 AND 6)

Settle in and invite God's presence through prayer, shared silence, lectio divina with Scripture, or a reflective reading.

1. How would you describe your relationship with technology these days? What are the joys, the frustrations, and the conundrums? Where have you seen technology contribute positively to your life and where do you experience bondage?

2. How do you respond to the statement quoted in this chapter: "Devices and social media apps are designed to become invasive, habit-forming and compulsive—if not a behavioral addiction at times. Many of the people who design digital technology and social media have publicly stated that their products are designed to be toxic, addicting and manipulative, depriving users of choice and free time through habit-forming feedback loops." Agree? Disagree? How might embracing a "tech shabbat" provide a way to practice freedom from this particular kind of bondage—at least one day a week—and maybe even transform your relationship with technology?

3. Have you ever tried to truly unplug from technology for a period of time? What was that like for you? Are you drawn to considering this as part of your sabbath practice, and might it work?

4. Did you try any of the experiments listed on page 62? What did you learn and observe?

5. Take time to reflect together on sabbath as delight. Go around your group and let each person share something that delights them—just because; no reason necessary. And then discuss how each of you might incorporate your specific delight into your sabbath practice.

6. How do you respond to the idea that sabbath itself is worship? Are you comfortable with this? If not, could you see yourself getting there over time?

SESSION 4 (READ AND REFLECT ON CHAPTER 7)

Settle in and invite God's presence through prayer, shared silence, lectio divina with Scripture, or a reflective reading.

1. When contemplating incorporating a sabbath practice into your life, it is important to be realistic about one's stage of life and what is actually possible! Take time for each person in the group to share the stage of life they are in right now as it relates to sabbath-keeping. What are the unique opportunities and challenges related to your specific season? Feel free to include seasonal considerations that may not be addressed in this chapter. This will take time, so let it. Listen with compassion; this is *not* a time to fix, problem-solve, or give advice. Just let each person talk about what life is like at whatever stage they are in, and also the desires and frustrations and possibilities contained within that season.

2. After each one has shared their season of life, reflect on what God's invitation to sabbath-keeping might look like in this season. What do you long for? Is there one idea you might want to try? Try to do something before you do everything.

If it feels appropriate, go around the circle (or break into smaller groups if you have more than eight people) and have each person pray a simple prayer for the person on their left—naming the season they have identified themselves to be in, the challenges that season represents, and any desire and intent they have expressed. In the simplest way possible and with few words, ask God to help them live into their heart's desire.

SESSION 5 (READ AND REFLECT ON CHAPTER 8)

Settle in and invite God's presence through prayer, shared silence, lectio divina with Scripture, or a reflective reading.

1. As you reflect on how sabbath forms us and what sabbath shapes *in* us, what are you most drawn to? What are you most in need of? If you already practice sabbath, what have you noticed about what sabbath forms in you?

2. How hard or easy is it for you to accept the limits that go along with being human (in general) and the limits that are more personal to being you? Do you agree or disagree with the statement that "there is something deeply spiritual about honoring the limitations of our existence as human, physical bodies in a world of time and space"? What has been your posture toward living within limits?

3. As you consider what to say no to on the sabbath (work, buying and selling, worry, technology), what seems hardest or raises questions for you?

4. As you consider saying yes to resting the body, replenishing the spirit, and restoring the soul on the sabbath, what will you add in each of those categories?

5. What is the best day for you and your family to take your sabbath? Are you able to keep it the same day on most weeks? Do you have any ideas for how you would like to signal the beginning and the end of sabbath? (This might take some experimentation.)

6. In the spirit of doing something before you do everything, set aside one day sometime in the future to plan and execute one sabbath day, and share your intention with the group. Use the sabbath worksheet in appendix C to create your plan for that day. (If you can't find a whole day, that's okay. Maybe you can agree on a sabbath afternoon or morning or evening.)

As a group, agree together on a date to come back together to debrief your experiences. If everyone can commit to planning and executing their sabbath within a month's time, reconvene in a month—or two or six—whatever the group can do.

Close by having someone read the poem on pages 115-16 out loud to help solidify the group's desire and intent.

SESSION 6 (READ THE EPILOGUE)

Settle in and invite God's presence through prayer, shared silence, lectio divina with Scripture, or a reflective reading.

1. The sole purpose of this session is for group members to debrief their sabbath experience with each other. Try hard to make this an open and accepting experience, with compassion. Don't rush. If sabbath-keeping feels for some like a nice idea that belongs in the "too hard for now file"—like it did for me for so many years—let it be okay because it is! Let God be the one to continue working and guiding each person's life and choices. Allow at least fifteen minutes for each person, couple, or family unit to share the following:

   • something about their planning process

   • what they tried

   • what went well

   • what didn't go quite so well

- what they learned
- whether they are feeling drawn to incorporate sabbath more regularly into their lives

2. Read and discuss Isaiah 30 and the obstacles to rest described in the epilogue. What obstacles to entering into God's rest did you experience as you were planning and entering into your sabbath time? Have you had any experience of rest saving you and keeping you? Or can you imagine how this might be true?

3. Be honest about the challenges and obstacles, and then reflect on the question, Is sabbath worth fighting for?

Close with a slow and meditative reading of these verses from Isaiah 58:13-14 and Hebrews 4:9-11. Read them as a blessing, read them as a promise, read them as a challenge.

If you refrain from trampling the sabbath,
    from pursuing your own interests on my holy day;
if you call the sabbath a delight
    and the holy day of the LORD honorable;
if you honor it, not going your own ways,
    serving your own interests, or pursuing your own affairs;
then you shall take delight in the LORD,
    and I will make you ride upon the heights of the earth;
I will feed you with the heritage of your ancestor Jacob,
    for the mouth of the LORD has spoken.

So then, a sabbath rest still remains for the people of God; for those who enter God's rest also cease from their labors as God did from his. Let us therefore make every effort to enter that rest.

NOTES

1. A WAKE-UP CALL

6   *Biking accident*: Ruth Haley Barton, *Sacred Rhythms: Arranging Our Lives for Spiritual Transformation* (Downers Grove, IL: InterVarsity Press, 2006), 130-31.

7   *If we do not allow*: Wayne Muller, *Sabbath: Finding Rest, Renewal, and Delight in Our Busy Lives* (New York: Bantam Books, 1999), 20.

8   *Henri Nouwen's seminal reflections*: Henri Nouwen, *The Way of the Heart: Desert Spirituality and Contemporary Ministry* (San Francisco: HarperSanFrancisco, 1991).

    It was wonderful: Ruth Haley Barton, *Invitation to Solitude and Silence: Experiencing God's Transforming Presence* (Downers Grove, IL: InterVarsity Press, 2004).

    A special quality of time: Tilden Edwards, *Sabbath Time* (Nashville: Upper Room Books, 2003), 18.

    Draw me into his invitation: I have attempted in this book to use gender-inclusive language to refer to God whenever possible. In just a few cases when the beauty and ease of using language cannot be preserved without using a pronoun, I have chosen to use the masculine pronoun. This does not mean I believe God is male; rather, I believe (and Scripture teaches us) that God incorporates male and female and at the same time transcends both.

9   *It was as if a whole people*: Abraham Joshua Heschel, *The Sabbath* (New York: Farrar, Straus and Giroux, 1951), 15.

12   *There is a word*: Heschel, *The Sabbath*, 15.

13   *God has invited me*: Ruth Haley Barton, *Invitation to Retreat: The Gift and Necessity of Time Away with God* (Downers Grove, IL: InterVarsity Press, 2018).

14   *Sabbath is the most precious*: Heschel, *The Sabbath*, 18.

2. BEGINNING WITH GOD

17   *A holiness in time*: Abraham Joshua Heschel, *The Sabbath: Its Meaning for Modern Man* (New York: Farrar, Straus and Giroux: 1951), 9.

18   *In the Torah it is written*: George Robinson, "Shabbat Rest and Renewal, Two Elements That Are the Essence of Shabbat," *MyJewishLearning.com*, accessed December 12, 2021, www.myjewishlearning.com/article/shabbat-rest-and-renewal/.

18   *After the six days of creation*: Heschel, *The Sabbath*, 22-23.

19   *Shabbat offers us a chance*: Robinson, "Shabbat Rest and Renewal."

21   *The Hebrew word* shabbat: David Alves, *A Sabbatical Primer for Pastors: How to Initiate and Navigate a Spiritual Renewal Leave* (Concord, NH: Paupakpress, 2014), 30-31.

22   *Sabbath honors the necessary wisdom*: Wayne Muller, *Sabbath: Finding Rest, Renewal, and Delight in Our Busy Lives* (New York: Bantam Books: 1999), 6-7.
       The principle involved: Tilden Edwards, *Sabbath Time* (Nashville, TN: Upper Room Books, 2003), 24.

23   *We know God not just in our conscious awareness*: Ron Rolheiser, "The Sacredness of Work," *Ron Rolheiser Newsletter*, June 4, 2006, https://ronrolheiser.com/the-sacredness-of-work/#.YecEwS1h2u4.

24   *In the book of Exodus*: Muller, *Sabbath: Finding Rest*, 36.

25   *The goal of all existence*: Norman Wirzba, *Living the Sabbath: Discovering Rhythms of Rest and Delight* (Grand Rapids, MI: Brazos Press, 2006), 30.

3. FINDING FREEDOM THROUGH RESISTANCE

27   *On that fateful Sunday*: Paul D. Patton and Robert H. Woods Jr., *Everyday Sabbath: How to Lead Your Dance with Media and Technology in Mindful and Sacred Ways* (Eugene, OR: Cascade Books, 2021), 3, 15.

28   *A tale of resistance*: Walter Brueggemann, *Sabbath as Resistance: Saying No to the Culture of Now* (Louisville, KY: Westminster John Knox Press, 2014).

29 *Into this system*: Brueggemann, *Sabbath as Resistance*, 5, emphasis added.

30 *The fourth commandment*: Brueggemann, *Sabbath as Resistance*, xiv.

32 *One of the most countercultural*: Kelly M. Kapic, *You're Only Human: How Your Limits Reflect God's Design and Why That's Good News* (Grand Rapids, MI: Brazos Press, 2022), 219.

33 *When we keep a Sabbath*: Dorothy Bass, *Receiving the Day: Christian Practices for Opening the Gift of Time* (San Francisco: Jossey-Bass, 2000), 63.
    A sabbath economy: Norman Wirzba, *Living the Sabbath: Discovering the Rhythms of Rest and Delight* (Grand Rapids, MI: Brazos Press, 2006), 123.

35 *When we rest*: Cole Arthur Riley, *This Here Flesh* (New York: Convergent, 2022), 156-57.

37 *We have no real access*: Richard Rohr, *Everything Belongs* (New York: Crossroad Publishing, 1999), 25.

4. DISCOVERING SABBATH IN COMMUNITY

39 *My instructor in Sabbath-keeping*: John M. Buchanan, "Sabbath-keeping: Work Is Not Finished Until It Is Enjoyed in Rest," *Christian Century,* July 18-25, 2001, www.christiancentury.org/article/2001-07/sabbath-keeping.
    Sabbath-keeping: Some key passages that establish rest as a major theme in Scripture: Genesis 1:31–2:3; Exodus 16 (entire chapter); Exodus 18:17-18, 22-23; Exodus 20:8-11; Exodus 23:10-13; Exodus 31:12-18; Exodus 34:21; Deuteronomy 5:12-15; Joshua 1:13-15; I Kings 8:56; Isaiah 14:7; Isaiah 30:15; Isaiah 58:13-14; Matthew 11:28-30; Matthew 12:6-8, 11-12; Mark 2:23-27; Hebrews 4:4-11. If you are so inclined, you can highlight in a particular color verses having to do with rest and literally see this vibrant thread in Scripture.

5. THE POWER OF UNPLUGGING

53 *Our phones are not accessories*: Sherry Turkle, "Stop Googling. Let's Talk," *The New York Times Sunday Review,* September 26, 2015, www.nytimes.com/2015/09/27/opinion/sunday/stop-googling-lets-talk.html.

54 *Digital formation versus spiritual formation*: Ed Cyzewski, *Reconnect: Spiritual Restoration from Digital Distraction* (Harrisonburg, VA: Herald Press, 2020), 36.

55 *March us directly*: Larry Rosen, *iDisorder: Understanding Our Obsession with Technology and Overcoming Its Hold on Us* (New York: Palgrave MacMillan, 2012), 8.

56 *Sabbath box*: Wayne Muller, *Sabbath: Finding Rest, Renewal, and Delight in Our Busy Lives* (New York: Bantam Books, 1999), 60.

57 *Having your phone nearby*: Tiffany Shlain, *24/6: The Power of Unplugging One Day a Week* (New York: Gallery Books, 2019), 43.

58 *Living 24/6 feels like magic*: Shlain, *24/6: The Power of Unplugging*, xii.

6. SABBATH AS DELIGHT

65 *The Sabbath is not dedicated*: Abraham Joshua Heschel, *Sabbath* (New York: Farrar, Straus and Giroux, 1951), 19.

69 *This vortex of dying and rising*: Dorothy Bass, *Receiving the Day: Christian Practices for Opening the Gift of Time* (San Francisco: Jossey-Bass, 2000), 88.

71 *Mend our tattered lives*: Heschel, *Sabbath*, 18.

73 *Something missing in my heart*: Hafiz, *The Gift: Poems by Hafiz*, Daniel Ladinsky, trans. (New York: Penguin Compass, 1999), 277.

8. SHAPING SABBATH

96 *Sabbath-keeping is a means of grace*: Some of this chapter first appeared in Ruth Haley Barton, *Sacred Rhythms: Arranging Our Lives for Spiritual Transformation* (Downers Grove, IL: InterVarsity Press, 2006), and Ruth Haley Barton, "Part 2 Leading in Rhythm: Rhythms of Work and Rest," Transforming Center, accessed February 21, 2022, https://transformingcenter.org/2013/07/part-2-leading-in-rhythm-rhythms-of-work-and-rest/.

Every seventh day a miracle: Abraham Joshua Heschel, *Sabbath* (New York: Farrar, Straus and Giroux, 1951), 83.

98 *Limits that are part of God's original act*: Kelly Kapic, *You're Only Human: How Your Limits Reflect God's Design and Why That's Good News* (Grand Rapids, MI: Brazos Press, 2022), 12.

99 *In an Instagram post*: Will Graves, "Biles Returns to Olympic Competition, Wins Bronze on Beam," AP News, August 3, 2021,

https://apnews.com/article/2020-tokyo-olympics-gymnastics
-simone-biles-8d61f4de9ec021860cda002f4eac5804.

99   *We're not just entertainment*: Graves, "Biles Returns to Olympic Competition.

100 *It was something*: Graves, "Biles Returns to Olympic Competition."
     We remain in awe of Simone: Graves, "Biles Returns to Olympic Competition."

101 *What does it mean*: Kapic, *You're Only Human*, 14.

103 *Actively resisting our culture*: Paul Patton and Robert Woods, *Everyday Sabbath: How to Lead Your Dance with Media and Technology in Mindful and Sacred Ways* (Eugene, OR: Cascade Books, 2021), 11.

104 *I take a defined break*: Robert A. Fryling, *The Leadership Ellipse: Shaping How We Lead by Who We Are* (Downers Grove, IL: InterVarsity Press, 2010), 38-39.

108 *Over dinner go around the table*: Dennis Linn, Sheila Fabricant Linn, and Matthew Linn, *Sleeping with Bread: Holding What Gives You Life* (Mahwah, NJ: Paulist Press, 1995).

109 *Because we do not rest we lose our way*: Wayne Muller, *Sabbath: Finding Rest, Renewal, and Delight in Our Busy Lives* (New York: Bantam Books, 1991), 1.

110 *Light a candle*: Muller, *Sabbath: Finding Rest*, 60-61.

112 *What does it mean*: Questions adapted from Kapic, *You're Only Human*, 14.
     Finite, particular, and rooted: Questions adapted from Kapic, *You're Only Human*, 14.

INTERLUDE: ON TIME

115 *On Time*: Ruth Haley Barton, *Sacred Rhythms: Arranging Our Lives for Spiritual Transformation* (Downers Grove, IL: InterVarsity Press, 2006).

10. WHEN SABBATH IS NOT ENOUGH

143 *The essence of Sabbatical*: A. Richard Bullock and Richard J. Bruesehoff, *Clergy Renewal: The Alban Guide to Sabbatical Planning* (Bethesda, MD: An Alban Institute Publication, 2000), 2.

145 *In their beginnings, many universities were connected to the church*: Bullock and Bruesehoff, *Clergy Renewal: The Alban Guide*, 4.

145 *The Transforming Center understands:* From a motion approved by the Transforming Center Board, May 2020.

148 *Why am I so tired:* Henri Nouwen, *Sabbatical Journey: The Diary of His Final Year* (New York: Crossroad Publishing Company, 1998), 13.
I am quite possessive: Nouwen, *Sabbatical Journey,* 13.

152 *The treadmill metaphor:* David C. Pohl, "Ministerial Sabbaticals," *Christian Ministry* 9, no.1 (January 1978): 8.

153 *Churches grow and thrive:* David C. Alves, *A Sabbatical Primer for Pastors* (self-published, 2014), 87.

155 *Everyone wins when clergy:* Roy Oswald, in Bullock and Bruesehoff, *Clergy Renewal: The Alban Guide,* viii.

11. MORE THAN A VACATION

159 *Jointly committing to sabbatical leave:* A. Richard Bullock and Richard J. Bruesehoff, *Clergy Renewal: The Alban Guide to Sabbatical Planning* (Bethesda, MD: Alban Institute, 2000), 12.
What they say they want: Bullock and Bruesehoff, *Clergy Renewal: The Alban Guide,* 18.

163 *Sabbatical is an intentional release:* David C. Alves, *A Sabbatical Primer for Pastors* (self-published, 2014), 31, 62.

165 *I have always been a cook:* Katherine May, *Wintering: The Power of Rest and Retreat in Difficult Times* (New York: Riverhead Books, 2020), 19.

166 *After I graduated:* B. J. Woodworth, application for sabbatical, April 14, 2015.

167 *It began with:* J. Taylor Haley, personal correspondence with author, used with permission.

169 *Myers-Briggs is a helpful model:* Robert Mulholland, *Invitation to a Journey: A Road Map for Spiritual Formation* (Downers Grove, IL: InterVarsity Press, 2016), 61-87.

12. A SEASON OF SPIRITUAL OPPORTUNITY

176 *I feel strange:* Henri Nouwen, *Sabbatical Journey: The Diary of His Final Year* (New York: Crossroad Publishing Company, 1998), 3.

177 *A compilation of excerpts:* Thomas Keating, *The Daily Reader for Contemplative Living: Excerpts from the Works of Father Thomas Keating,* compiled by S. Stephanie Iachetta (New York: Continuum, 2003).

186   *Be patient*: Rainer Maria Rilke, *Letters to a Young Poet* (New York: W.W. Norton, 1934), 35.

187   *Ministry re-entry*: David Alves, *A Sabbatical Primer for Pastors* (self-published, 2014), 79.

189   *Since my first sabbatical I have learned*: A. Richard Bullock and Richard J. Bruesehoff, *Clergy Renewal: The Alban Guide to Sabbatical Planning* (Alban Institute Publication, 2000), 54.

13. SETTING BOUNDARIES

194   *A modern-day lynching*: James Cone, *The Cross and the Lynching Tree* (New York: Orbis Books, 2011), 7.

196   *David Alves's clarification about the sabbath*: David Alves, *A Sabbatical Primer for Pastors* (self-published, 2014), 30-31.

199   *Say no to everything but writing*: Henri Nouwen, *Sabbatical Journey: The Diary of His Final Year* (New York: Crossroad Publishing Company, 1998), vii.
      Most of the day I have been busy: Nouwen, *Sabbatical Journey*, 16, 145.

203   *What needs to be guarded*: Henri Nouwen, *The Way of the Heart: Desert Spirituality and Contemporary Ministry* (New York: Harper SanFrancisco, 1981), 30.

206   *This moment does feel different*: Phaedra Blocker, personal communication with author, June 2020.

207   *To let go of my relevant self*: Henri Nouwen, *In the Name of Jesus: Reflections on Christian Leadership* (New York: Crossroad Publishing, 1989), 28.

208   *Through the empty branches the sky remains*: Rainer Maria Rilke, *Rilke's Book of Hours: Love Poems to God*, trans. Anita Barrows and Joanna Macy (New York: Riverhead Books, 1996), 96.

INTERLUDE: A BLESSING FOR SABBATICAL TIME

211   *A meditation on Psalm 46:10*: First part adapted from Henri Nouwen, *Spiritual Direction: Wisdom for the Long Walk of Faith* (New York: Harper One, 2015), 82-84.

214   *For your sake*: Adapted from Bart Kelso, "A Liturgy of Sending and Blessing," The Union Church of Waban, July 30, 2015.

EPILOGUE

215 *More than Israel has kept Shabbat*: "Shabbat: What is Shabbat?" Jewish Virtual Library, accessed January 31, 2021, www.jewish virtuallibrary.org/what-is-shabbat-jewish-sabbath.

220 *The mind that comes to rest is tended*: Wendell Berry, *A Timbered Choir: The Sabbath Poems 1979-1997* (New York: Counterpoint, 1998), 7.

GRATITUDE

222 *The world aches for the generosity*: Wayne Muller, *Sabbath: Finding Rest, Renewal, and Delight in Our Busy Life* (New York: Bantam Books, 1999), 11.

APPENDIX B: PREPARING FOR REENTRY

225 *Rule of life*: Ruth Haley Barton, *Sacred Rhythms* (Downers Grove, IL: InterVarsity Press, 2006), chapter 9.

BECOMING A SABBATH COMMUNITY

233 *Devices and social media apps*: Ed Cyzewski, *Reconnect: Spiritual Restoration from Digital Distraction* (Harrisonburg, VA: Herald Press, 2020), 36.

BIBLIOGRAPHY

THE SABBATH LIFE IS LIKE a multifaceted diamond that flashes different fiery colors depending on the light, the backdrop, and how you turn it. It is not possible for one work to capture all the fire, so I am including a bibliography of resources I have benefited from in my study and practice of sabbath-keeping. So enjoy! But please remember that reading about the sabbath life—as pleasurable as that is—is not the same thing as practicing it. My prayer is that whatever you choose to read will support a true and life-altering practice.

SABBATH

Baab, Lynne M. *Sabbath Keeping: Finding Freedom in the Rhythms of Rest.* Downers Grove, IL: InterVarsity Press, 2005.

Bass, Dorothy C. *Receiving the Day: Christian Practices for Opening the Gift of Time.* San Francisco: Jossey-Bass Publishers, 2000.

Berry, Wendell. *A Small Porch: Sabbath Poems 2014 and 2015.* New York: Counterpoint, 2016.

——. *This Day: Collected and New Sabbath Poems.* New York: Counterpoint, 2014.

——. *A Timbered Choir: The Sabbath Poems 1979-1997.* New York: Counterpoint, 1998.

Brueggemann, Walter. *Sabbath as Resistance: Saying No to the Culture of Now.* Louisville, KY: Westminster John Knox Press, 2014.

Buchanan, Mark. *The Rest of God: Restoring Your Soul by Restoring Sabbath.* Nashville, TN: Thomas Nelson Publishers, 2006.

Dana, MaryAnn McKibben. *Sabbath in the Suburbs: A Family's Experiment with Holy Time*. St. Louis, Missouri: Chalice Press, 2012.

Edwards, Tilden. *Sabbath Time*. Nashville, TN: Upper Room Books, 1992/2003.

Heschel, Abraham Joseph. *The Sabbath*. New York: Farrar, Straus, and Giroux, 1951.

Muller, Wayne. *Sabbath: Finding Rest, Renewal, and Delight in Our Busy Lives*. New York: Bantam Books, 1999.

Wirzba, Norman. *Living the Sabbath: Discovering the Rhythms of Rest and Delight*. Grand Rapids, MI: Brazos Press, 2006.

SABBATICAL

Alves, David C. *A Sabbatical Primer for Pastors: How to Initiate and Navigate a Spiritual Renewal Leave*. Self-published, 2014.

Bullock, A. Richard and Richard J. Bruesehoff. *Clergy Renewal: The Alban Guide to Sabbatical Planning*. Bethesda, MD: An Alban Institute Publication, 2000.

Nouwen, Henri J. M. *Sabbatical Journey: The Diary of His Final Year*. New York: Crossroad Publishing Company, 2014.

TECHNOLOGY

Carr, Nicholas. *The Shallows: What the Internet Is Doing to Our Brains*. New York: W. W. Norton and Co., 2010.

Cyzewski, Ed. *Reconnect: Spiritual Restoration from Digital Distraction*. Harrisonburg, VA: Herald Press, 2020.

Harris, Michael. *The End of Absence: Reclaiming What We've Lost in a World of Constant Connection*. New York: Current, 2014.

Patton, Paul D. and Robert H. Woods Jr. *Everyday Sabbath: How to Lead Your Dance with Media and Technology in Mindful and Sacred Ways*. Eugene, OR: Cascade Books, 2021.

Rosen, Larry. *iDisorder: Understanding Our Obsession with Technology and Overcoming Its Hold on Us*. New York: Palgrave Macmillan, 2012.

Shlain, Tiffany. *24/6: The Power of Unplugging One Day a Week*. New York: Gallery Books, 2019.

Turkle, Sherry. *Alone Together: Why We Expect More from Technology and Less from Each Other*. New York: Basic Books, 2011.

"The best thing any of us can bring to leadership is our own transforming selves. That is the journey I am committed to and it is the journey to which you are invited as well."

—Ruth Haley Barton

Visit *transformingcenter.org* to
- Discover free resources written by Ruth
- Listen to Ruth's podcast
- Subscribe to Ruth's blog

Ruth has been a student, practitioner, and leader in the area of Christian spirituality and spiritual formation for leaders for over twenty years. Encountering the richness of the broader Christian tradition has led Ruth to reclaim practices and experiences that spiritual seekers down through the ages have used to open themselves to God's transforming work.

Join Ruth on Retreat

A sought-after teacher, preacher, and retreat leader, you will always find Ruth teaching and leading the Transforming Center's two-year Transforming Community experience—a practice-based spiritual formation journey for pastors and leaders offered in nine quarterly retreats. For more information visit transformingcenter.org.

 TRANSFORMING | Resources®

More from Ruth Haley Barton

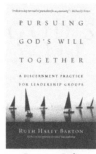

Strengthening the Soul
of Your Leadership

Pursuing God's
Will Together

Longing for More

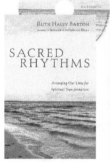

Sacred Rhythms

Sacred Rhythms DVD
curriculum

Invitation to Solitude
and Silence

Invitation to Retreat

Life Together in Christ

To learn more about transforming resources, communities, and events, visit

transformingcenter.org

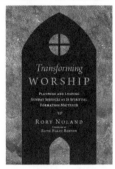

Transforming Worship

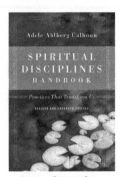

Spiritual Disciplines
Handbook

Invitations from God

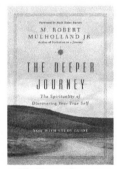

The Deeper Journey

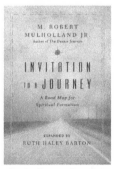

Invitation to a Journey

To learn more about transforming resources, communities, and events, visit

transformingcenter.org

CPSIA information can be obtained
at www.ICGtesting.com
Printed in the USA
JSHW060708301022
32233JS00001B/1/J